D1384914

THE
AMERICAN
CHECKER PLAYER'S
HANDBOOK

CHECKER BOARD WITH MEN

THE AMERICAN CHECKER PLAYER'S HANDBOOK

A Modern and Practical Work or the
Science of Checkers for Beginners, and
a Reliable Authority for the Advanced
Player and Expert

By ERROLL A. SMITH

Professional Match Player; Simultaneous Exhibition
Player; Former Atlantic City Champion; Secretary
Philadelphia Chess and Checker Club; Secretary
Pennsylvania Checker Association

THE JOHN C. WINSTON COMPANY
PHILADELPHIA
TORONTO

TABLE OF CONTENTS

PREFACE

The American Checker Player's Handbook is a comprehensive and entertaining work on the Game of Checkers, including its History, Laws, Instructions for playing Two-Move-Restriction Games with annotations, the so-called Barred Openings, and a selection of useful problems for the student.

In addition to the foregoing, many new features are introduced. These unique features include the Seven "Secrets" of Success, as practiced by the world's experts; the Definition of Major and Minor Variations, together with the Theory, Study and Practice of the Game under the Seven Master Openings System; the Playing Charts, the Transposition Tables; a pithy treatise on Problem Solving; Lessons in Finishing, and the Special Game Indexes.

The various games and variations contained herein are the last word in up-to-date play of the foremost masters throughout the world, which have been subjected to careful selection and close analysis, only the soundest being incorporated in this work.

7

The main body of the work is in reality a synthesis for all grades of players, that simplifies the study and practice of the game to an extent never previously considered possible.

Its clearly explained method of study and application will enable the beginner to attain a proficiency in playing, in a short time, not to be accomplished with any other book treating of the game, as the openings and necessary subsequent play are easily memorized.

Many old-time games with their variations are dispensed with under the methods used in this book, while thousands of variations are eliminated by the adoption of lines of play that preclude their introduction. Many new variations and so-called improvements may be summarily discarded, as they usually prove to be but deviations that go back to previously known play or that blend into established lines.

At once fascinating and instructive, this book simplifies the game, instead of making it more complex, and while a constant source of information and instruction to the beginner, it will prove a welcome addition to the library of the advanced checkerist.

ERROLL A. SMITH.

A BRIEF HISTORY OF THE GAME

The origin of the Game of Checkers or Draughts, like that of Chess, is lost in the mists of antiquity, but from fleeting references made to it in ancient manuscripts, together with discoveries unearthed in scientific excavations, man has been enabled to trace it back to about 6000 years B. C. Authentic information has definitely established the fact that the game was known and practiced in Egypt at least as early as that date, if not earlier, although the probabilities are the game was played in a much cruder form, with the pieces of different appearance than those now used and with a greater number of squares.

The game, in much of its present form, was a familiar form of amusement among the Moors at the time of the conquest of the City of Granada. A similar game is enjoyed by the Chinese and by the aborigines of New Zealand. The extreme age of the game may be appreciated when it is remembered that ordinary playing-cards were originated in China as recently as the year 1120 A. D.

In the Royal Library of Madrid reposes the first book on checkers ever printed. This book

9

made its appearance in the City of Valencia in the year 1547 A. D.   Printed books on the game then appeared in France and Germany, and a little more than two hundred years after the original publication in Spanish, appeared the first Checker Book printed in English, written by William Payne of London, England, in the year 1756.

Since that time the literature of the game has been steadily increasing, both as regards volume and knowledge, until at the present time there are hundreds of books concerning the game, ranging in contents from the veriest beginner's primary lessons to the large and expensive National Tourney Books which are placed on the market following every big tourney.

The Press has been no small factor in the growth of the game, featuring special checker columns, carrying the news of the game, problems and criticisms, to say nothing of the numerous checker magazines which are published from time to time.

Checkers is an ancient and honorable game, contributing to the education and amusement of thousands upon thousands of players of all grades throughout the world.   It is the highest type of mental recreation.

COMPARISON OF STYLES

THE UNRESTRICTED, OR
GO-AS-YOU-PLEASE GAME

This is the earliest known style of playing the game of which we have record, the 11 15, 23 19 opening formation assuming and maintaining the lead in this style to the present day. One might even safely state that he plays "11 15 Checkers" rather than Go-As-You-Please Checkers, as even superficial observation will show that the greatest advocates of the Go-As-You-Please style are ardent devotees of 11 15 as an opening move.

While it is not our desire to create the impression that the game is exhausted under this style of play, a glance in any textbook of old standard openings will forcefully illustrate the fact that the game could never attain its highest development when eleven unrestricted or named openings all emanate from 11 15, 23 19. The constant repetition of the opening moves led naturally to the repeating of subsequent moves, until whole games were but duplicates of each other.

To cite an example, a match of seventy-two games was arranged between Messrs. Wyllie and

Martins in 1872, at that time the two foremost masters of the silent game. In that match the opening moves 11 15, 23 19, were adopted in fifty-five games of the seventy-two played, and thirty-five of these were exact duplicates of each other. We leave it to the reader to draw his own conclusions regarding unrestricted play.

Two-Move Restriction

This style of play was first introduced in England and Scotland in the closing years of the nineteenth century, with the object of avoiding the constant repetition of 11 15, 23 19 as opening moves.

In this it was entirely successful, as it at once became necessary to have at least a knowledge of all the opening moves on the board. This in turn increased a player's cross-board ability to an extent heretofore undreamed of, the only serious fault being the abandoning of the so-called Barred Openings as being too weak for further consideration.

Since the 1905 British-American International Match this style has been steadily increasing in popularity in America, until now it is the style adopted by all good players throughout the world.

In 1920 the four so-called Barred Openings were voted into use at the Fourth American

National Tourney. This evidence of re-awakened interest in them has created a worldwide discussion as to their merits and demerits, and at the present writing the players of all countries are working hard on them with a view to retaining them in all individual, city, state, and national matches and tourneys.

INSTRUCTIONS

The Game of Checkers is played by two players on a board of sixty-four squares, thirty-two light and thirty-two dark, with two sets of twelve men each, of adverse colors. In the Two-Move Restriction style of play a pack of forty-seven cards, one for each opening, is also used, each card having upon it the first move for Black and the first move for White. At the commencement of the game the pack is shuffled and one card drawn, each player being restricted to making his first opening move as called for on the card drawn, after which each player may, in turn, move as his fancy dictates. A card is used but once during a match.

In playing, the dark squares of the board are used, while in diagrams of positions or problems the pictured board is turned around and the white squares used, so that the pieces may show up plainly. The following diagram represents the board with the pieces placed for play at the commencement of the game.

It will be noted the Black pieces are placed for the opponent, White pieces for the player:

Black—1, 2, 3, 4, 5, 6, 7, 8, 9, 10, 11, 12

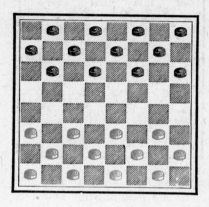

White—21, 22, 23, 24, 25, 26, 27, 28, 29, 30, 31, 32

As shown, Black occupies the first twelve squares on the board, and White the last twelve, eight squares remaining vacant. The board being numbered (considering only the dark squares) from 1 to 32, the numbers being read, as shown on the accompanying diagram, from left to right on each succeeding line. As the pieces change places at the beginning of each game, the numbers, of course, change places also, or to make it clearer, turn the board around, so that your opponent has the side you just had. The numbered board:

The games in this book are set down in five columns, and are read starting at the top of the first column—down, then continue at the top of the second column, etc.   As Black moves first, the first set of figures are Black's opening move. 12 16 meaning Black moves the piece on square 12 to square 16.   The next set of figures are White's opening move, 24 20 meaning White moves the piece on square 24 to square 20, etc. Figures beside the moves indicate variations, and letters mean notes below the game.   Stars mean best moves, or sometimes the only move to win or draw, as the case may be.   Each player in turn moves one of his pieces to the right or left along the diagonal on which it stands, one square at a time, in a forward direction only.   Upon reaching the last row on the opposite side of the board, either by moving, or in capturing a piece, they are crowned by placing another piece of like color on top of them, and are then known as Kings, and may be played forward or backward one square at a time, as the limits of the board permit. Aside from their power to move backward or jump (capture) backward, they are in all respects the same as an ordinary piece.

In capturing, the men capture in the direction in which they move, by leaping over any opposing piece of adverse color that lies directly in front of it on either diagonal, providing there is a vacant square directly behind the piece captured for the capturing piece to light upon.

A capturing *piece* may take from one to three pieces in one move, providing there are vacant squares behind each one as described above. The capturing piece must stop upon arriving in the opponent's king row, as this completes the move, and he may not be moved again until crowned. A capturing *King* may take as many pieces as there are vacant squares behind them, and being a King does not have to stop upon reaching the opponent's king-row, but if there are more pieces still in take, may continue to capture them. All pieces or Kings captured are immediately removed from the board. When there are two ways of capturing, the player may take his choice. The final object of the game is

2

to capture or confine all of your opponent's pieces. The player whose pieces are first brought to this state loses the game.   Sometimes an opponent's pieces are so placed that he can move but cannot be stopped.   This makes a perpetual draw.   See page 109.

SEVEN SECRETS OF SUCCESS

1. Always try to command the center of the board and squares 14 and 19. They are "key" squares and their occupation or control leads to a superior game.

2. Attack your opponent's double corner, and weaken it by the exchange of pieces whenever possible. In some instances a well-filled double corner is better than a "bridge."

3. The "bridge" is formed by the pieces on squares 1 and 3 when playing Black, and 30 and 32 when playing White. Try to break your opponent's bridge and preserve your own.

4. Never make a move without a definite purpose in view or the knowledge that this book gives it as a good move. Try to seek the reason for every move played against you.

5. All the moves in the Games have an object behind them. When playing with an opponent, if he deviates from the play you know, study the position carefully for an advantage, and look up his play at the first opportunity.

6. Observe games between good players whenever possible, and when more experienced, record

your own, and compare them. Practice solving problems, and memorize the solutions to the useful positions given in the back of this book.

7. Memorize the Playing Charts, evolve other transpositions yourself, and acquire a library of Checker books. It would also be helpful to take a magazine and read a newspaper column on the game and attend all the tourneys and matches you can.

THE MOVE AND ITS CHANGES

THE MOVE

There is supposed to be a mysterious something which enables the book-player to play a wonderful game. This, of course, is not the case, but a thorough knowledge of the Move and its changes will materially improve any player's end game. The most easily understood explanation of what is meant by "having the move" is to place a black piece on square 3 and a white piece on square 30. Now whichever piece is moved first, wins. We decide on Black, and move 3 7. White is then moved 30 26, Black is moved 7 10, and if White then goes 26 23, Black wins by 10 15, and if White goes 26 22, Black wins by 10 14. Black had the move on his turn to play. In other words, "He has the move who has the last move."

CALCULATION OF THE MOVE

For this purpose the playing squares of the board are divided into two systems of four columns each. One system consists of the four columns that end in Black's king-row with the squares 1, 2, 3, and 4. The other system consists of the four columns that end in White's king-row with the squares 29, 30, 31, and 32. The student will note that Black's system of columns ends in white squares on White's side of the board, and *vice versa.*

To Determine Who Has the "Move"

When it is your turn to play, count all the pieces in your own system, regardless of color. If the sum is odd, you have the "move," if even, "the move" lies with your opponent. This applies only when the pieces of each opponent are equal. To alter the "move," an exchange of odd pieces is required, as one for one, or three for three; but one of the capturing pieces must also be taken or the rule will not apply.

To determine who has the move when the pieces are unequal, as three kings to two, or four to three, imagine the board being equally divided vertically. Now count as before; if the sum is odd, you have the move (it being your turn to play) only on the half of the board in which your double corner lies; if even, you have the move only on that half of the board in which your single corner lies. Refer to Seventh Position as an example.

Influence of a "Locked" Piece on the "Move"

We term a piece "locked" when it is prevented from moving forward by pieces on adjacent squares immediately in front of it. A simple example is Black on 28 and White on 32, with Black to move. Black's piece is "locked." In counting the move with one locked piece of either color on the board the result will be found directly opposite to the established rule. Locking another piece, releasing the locked piece, or an exchange will change the result.

THE STANDARD LAWS

THE STANDARD BOARD

1. The Standard Board must be of light and dark squares, not less than fourteen and one-half inches, nor more than sixteen inches across said squares. The board shall be placed for play so that the bottom corner square on the left hand shall be black.

THE STANDARD MEN

2. The Standard Men, technically described as Black and White, must be light and dark (say red and white, preferably, or black and white), turned, and round, and not less than one and one-eighth inches, nor more than one and one-fourth inches in diameter.

PLACING THE MEN

3. The men shall be placed on the black squares. The black men shall invariably be placed upon the real or supposed first twelve squares of the board; the white men upon the last twelve squares.

ORDER OF PLAY

4. Each player shall play alternately with black and white men, lots shall be cast for the color only once—viz., at the commencement of a match—the winner to have the choice of taking either black or white men. The first move shall invariably be made by the player having the black men.

TIME LIMIT FOR MOVING

5. At the end of five minutes (if the move has not previously been made), "time" must be called in a distinct manner by the person appointed for the purpose; and if the move be not completed on the expiration of another minute, the game shall be adjudged as lost through improper delay. When there is only one way of taking one or more pieces, "time" shall be called at the end of one minute, and if the move be not completed at the expiration of another minute, the game shall be adjudged as lost through improper delay.

ARRANGING THE MEN DURING A GAME

6. Either player is entitled, on giving intimation, to arrange his own or his opponent's pieces properly on the squares. After the move has been made, however, if either player touch or arrange any piece without giving intimation, he shall be cautioned for the first offence, and shall forfeit the game for any subsequent act of the kind.

Touch and Move

7. After the pieces have been arranged, if the person whose turn it is to play touch one, he must either play it or forfeit the game. When the piece is not playable, he is penalized according to the preceding law. If any part of a playable piece be played over the angle of the square on which it is stationed, the play must be completed in that direction. A capturing play, as well as an ordinary one, is completed when the hand of the player is withdrawn from the piece played, even though one or more pieces should have been taken. When taking, if a player remove one of his own pieces, he cannot replace it; but his opponent can either play or insist upon his replacing it.

False or Improper Moves

8. Either player making a false or improper move instantly forfeits the game to his opponent, without another move being made.

The Huff or Blow

9. The Huff or Blow is for a player to remove from the board any of his opponent's pieces that might or should have captured any of his

pieces. It never constitutes a play, and should be employed before moving his own piece. **The player has the power to Huff, compel the take, or let it remain.** (This law is now practically discarded as being childish, all good players insisting upon a piece being taken.)

Crowning the Men

10. When a single piece first reaches any of the squares on the extreme opposite end of the board (the opponent's king-row), it becomes a king, and must be crowned before another move is made by either player. It can then be moved backwards or forwards, one square at a time, as the limits of the board permit. The king must be crowned by the player having the opposite pieces.

Drawn Games

11. A game is drawn when neither of the players can force a win. If one player appears stronger than the other, that party is required to complete the win or show a decided advantage to the satisfaction of the referee within forty of his own moves—to be counted from the point at which notice was given—failing in which he must relinquish the game as drawn.

Conduct of the Players and Spectators

12. Anything tending to distract or annoy a player is strictly forbidden—unnecessarily delay-

ing to move a piece touched, or other ignorant
practices by the other player.   Any player acting
in this manner after having been warned shall
forfeit the game.   While play is pending neither
player shall leave the room without sufficient
reason or having the other's consent or company.

Any spectator giving warning or comment in
any manner on a game, whether playing or
pending, shall be ordered from the room during
the match—play to be discontinued until such
offending party retires.

MATCH GAMES

13. A match between equals, wins and draws
to count, should consist of an even number of
games, so that each player may have the first
move the same number of times.   A card shall
be drawn but once, and both sides played.

TOURNEY AND TEAM MATCHES

14. Tourney and team matches should consist
of an equal number of games between each pair
of players, regardless of the number of players in
the tourney, or on each team.   See Rule 13.

EXCESSIVE TIE SCORES

15. Tourneys played under the straight
"knock-out" style of play should consist of as
many additional sets of two games as are found

necessary to eliminate one of the contestants, to prevent excessive tie scores. In the double knock-out style of play both players are usually penalized a half-life and both passed on into the succeeding round.

Enforcement of the Laws

16. All players and tourney committees are equally bound to exact the enforcement of the penalties provided for any breach of the foregoing rules.

Unforeseen Disputes

17. In tourneys the decision of the Tourney Committee shall be final. In matches, when any dispute arises not satisfactorily settled by the preceding laws, the facts shall be submitted to a disinterested party, having a knowledge of the game, whose decision shall be final.

THE THEORY

For the purpose of rapid development it is assumed that there are seven Master Openings and four (or less) Major Variations to each opening.

Only one of the seven White replies to Black's opening move can form a Master Opening. The remaining opening moves form Major Variations, or allow the formation of other Master Openings.

This classification will be found a short and easy method of committing the openings to memory.

Refer to the Playing Charts.

THE STUDY

To condense the forty-seven Two-Move Restriction Openings to the Seven Master Openings and Major Variations, and whenever possible, where it will allow the formation of a sound game, to employ one line of play for two or more opening formations: this tends to simplify the game and reduce the amount of playing that has previously been necessary to play a good strong game.

Refer to the Transposition Tables.

THE PRACTICE

When playing with the Black pieces, confine your opponent to a line of attack you are familiar with.

When playing the White pieces, confine your opponent to a line of defense you are familiar with *in the attack which Black elects to play.*

Refer to the Games.

MAJOR VARIATIONS

Major Variations arise from those moves which do not form Master Openings. There are four or less variations to every Master Opening. There are less when the original sequence of moves leading to a given formation may be arrived at from transposition.

To illustrate—Major Variation 1-A *would be* 12 16, 24 19, but Black, on his second move, plays 8 12, making the position identical at that point with Major Variation 2-A, by simply transposing the first two moves.

The student's interests are best served by presenting the Master Openings and Major Variations in the Playing Charts and all transpositions in the Transposition Tables, instead of listing in consecutive order all Black moves with each White reply in order.

MINOR VARIATIONS

These are lines of play departing from the Master Openings or Major Variations, and these are dealt with in the Transposition Tables only to the extent necessary to show the opening moves.   Minor Variations of 11 15, 23 19 are presented without notes, in the form of named openings that show a model line of play on each, following Master Opening 3, so as to acquaint the student with their formation.

PLAYING CHARTS

THE MASTER OPENINGS AND MAJOR VARIATIONS

Open. 1	1-A	1-B	1-C
12 16	12 16	12 16	12 16
24 20	23 19	22 17	21 17
8 12	16 23	16 19	9 13
28 24	27 18	24 15	25 21
9 14	11 16	11 18	16 19
22 18	22 17	23 14	23 16
see	see	see	see
p. 43	p. 46	p. 66	p. 68

Open. 2	2-A	2-B	2-C	2-D
11 16	11 16	11 16	11 16	11 16
24 20	24 19	23 19	22 17	21 17
16 19	8 11	16 23	16 19	10 15
23 16	22 18	26 19	24 15	17 14
12 19	10 14	9 14	10 19	9 18
22 18	26 22	27 23	23 16	23 14
see	see	see	see	see
p. 71	p. 73	p. 74	p. 76	p. 78

Open. 3	3-A	3-B	3-C	3-D
11 15	11 15	11 15	11 15	11 15
23 19	24 19	23 18	22 18	21 17
9 13	15 24	8 11	15 22	9 13

(Continued on page 34.)

Open. 3	3-A	3-B	3-C	3-D
22 18	28 19	27 23	25 18	25 21
15 22	9 14	10 14	10 15	8 11
25 18	22 18	23 19	18 11	17 14
see	see	see	see	see
p. 83	p. 87	p. 89	p. 91	p. 92

Open. 4	4-A	4-B	4-C
10 15	10 15	10 15	10 15
23 18	24 20	24 19	23 19
7 10	15 19	15 24	6 10
27 23	23 16	28 19	22 17
3 7	12 19	6 10	1 6
see	see	see	see
p. 98	p. 102	p. 103	p. 105

Open. 5	5-A	5-B	5-C	5-D
10 14	10 14	10 14	10 14	10 14
22 17	24 20	24 19	23 19	23 18
7 10	11 15	6 10	11 16	14 23
17 13	22 17	22 17	26 23	27 18
3 7	6 10	9 13	9 13	12 16
see	see	see	see	see
p. 110	p. 112	p. 116	p. 118	p. 122

Open. 6	6-A
9 14	9 14
22 18	23 18
5 9	14 23
24 20	27 18
11 16	12 16
see	see
p. 126	p. 128

For other White replies to 9 14, refer to the Transposition Tables.

Open. 7	7–A	7–B	7–C	7–D
9 13	9 13	9 13	9 13	9 13
22 18	24 20	24 19	23 18	22 17
6 9	11 15	11 15	5 9	13 22
25 22	22 17	28 24	26 23	25 18
1 6	13 22	6 9	11 16	6 9
see	see	see	see	see
p. 133	p. 137	p. 141	p. 143	p. 146

MISCELLANEOUS OPENING FORMATIONS

F–1	F–2	F–3	F–4	F–5
12 16	12 16	12 16	12 16	12 16
24 19	23 18	22 17	22 17	21 17
16 20	8 12	16 20	8 12	9 13
22 18	18 14	17 13	25 22	24 20
11 15	9 18	9 14	4 8	8 12
18 11	22 8	25 22	17 13	25 21
8 24	4 11	8 12	16 20	3 8

F–6	F–7	F–8	F–9	F–10
11 16	11 16	11 15	11 15	10 14
22 17	21 17	24 20	24 20	24 20
10 15	9 14	8 11	10 14	6 10
23 18	25 21	28 24	22 18	22 18
15 22	16 19	3 8	15 22	11 15
25 18	24 15	23 19	25 18	18 11
9 14	10 19		6 10	8 15

TRANSPOSITION TABLES

11 16	9 13	12 16	11 16	9 13
24 20	23 18	23 18	23 19	21 17
8 11	12 16	9 13	16 23	12 16
28 24	24 20	24 20	27 18	
	8 12	8 12	12 16	
	28 24	28 24		
Refer	Op. 1	Op. 1		
to Op. 1	Note D	Note D	1-A	1-C

11 15	9 14	12 16	12 16	12 16
24 20	22 18	24 19	23 18	22 18
15 19	11 16	8 12	16 20	8 12
	18 9		24 19	24 19
	5 14		10 14	10 14
	24 20		26 23	26 22
	16 19		8 12	16 20
Refer				
to Op. 2	Op. 2	2-A	2-A	2-A

12 16	11 16	11 16	11 16	10 14
22 18	23 18	22 18	22 18	24 19
16 20	16 20	10 14	8 11	11 16
24 19	24 19	24 19	24 19	22 18
10 14	10 14	16 20		
26 22	26 23	26 22		
8 12	8 11	8 11		
Refer				
to 2-A	2-A	2-A	2-A	2-A

36

11 15	10 15	10 15	9 13	9 14
22 17	22 17	21 17	23 19	24 19
15 19	11 16	11 16	11 15	11 15
				27 24
Refer				Var. 1
to 2-C	2-D	2-D	Op. 3	Op. 3

---

9 14	10 14	10 14	10 14	9 14
23 19	24 19	22 18	22 18	22 18
11 15	6 10	6 10	11 15	6 9
27 23	22 18	24 19	18 11	24 19
Refer	11 15	Colors	8 15	Colors
to	Colors	Rev.	Colors	Rev.
Var. 1	Rev. v. 1	var. 1	Rev. v. 1	var. 1
Op. 3	Op. 3	Op. 3	Op. 3	Op. 3

---

9 14	9 14	10 15	11 15	11 15
23 19	22 17	22 17	22 17	22 17
11 15	11 15	7 10	9 14	7 11
22 17	23 19	23 19	23 19	23 19
7 11				9 14
Refer				25 22
to				
Var. 3	Var. 3	Var. 3	Var. 3	Var.3
Op. 3	Op. 3	Op. 3	Op. 3	Op. 3

10 15	10 14	10 14	10 14	10 14
23 19	23 19	23 19	22 17	22 17
7 10	7 10	6 10	7 10	6 1C
22 17	22 17	22 17	23 19	23 19
9 14	11 15	11 15	11 15	11 15
25 22	17 13	17 13	17 13	17 13
Refer	2 7	2 6	2 7	2 6
to				
Var. 3	Var. 6	Var. 6	Var. 6	Var. 6
Op. 3	Op. 3	Op. 3	Op. 3	Op. 3

---

9 14	9 14	9 14	9 14	11 15
22 17	23 19	22 17	23 19	21 17
6 9	5 9	5 9	11 15	8 11
23 19	26 23	23 19	26 23	25 21
11 15				3 8
Refer				23 19
to				
Var. 6	Var. 8	Var. 8	Var. 8	Var. 9
Op. 3	Op. 3	Op. 3	Op. 3	Op. 3

---

11 15	10 15	9 14	10 15	11 15
21 17	21 17	24 19	24 19	23 19
7 11	7 10	11 15	15 24	8 11
25 21	25 21	22 18	28 19	27 23
3 7	3 7	15 24	9 14	4 8
23 19	23 19	18 9	22 18	23 18
Refer		5 14		
to		28 19		
Var. 9	Var. 9			
Op. 3	Op. 3	3-A	3-A	3-B

10 15	9 13	11 15	12 16	10 15
22 18	21 17	23 18	23 18	22 17
15 22	11 15	7 11	10 15	6 10
25 18				23 19
11 15				
Refer			Part	
to			Two	
3-C	3-D	Op. 4	Op. 4	4-C
11 15	9 14	9 13	9 14	9 14
24 20	24 19	23 19	24 20	24 19
10 14	6 9	11 16	5 9	5 9
22 17	22 17	26 23	22 18	22 18
Refer				Part
to				Two
5-A	5-B	5-C	Op. 6	Op. 6
11 15	11 15	11 15	11 16	10 15
24 20	22 17	22 18	23 18	22 18
9 13	9 13	15 22	9 13	15 22
22 17	24 20	25 18	26 23	25 18
Refer		9 13	5 9	6 10
to		24 19		
7-A	7-A	7-B	7-C	7-D
12 16	12 16	11 16	12 16	12 16
24 19	22 18	23 18	22 17	21 17
16 20	16 20	8 11	16 20	8 12
22 18	24 19		17 13	17 13
			9 14	16 20
			25 22	22 17
Refer			8 12	9 14
to			22 17	25 21
F-1	F-1	F-2	F-3	F-3

12 16	11 16	11 16	11 16	11 16
21 17	22 17	22 17	21 17	21 17
9 14	16 20	8 11	8 11	9 14
25 21	17 13	17 13	17 13	25 21
16 20	9 14	16 20	16 20	16 20
17 13	25 22	21 17	22 17	17 13
8 12	8 11	9 14	9 14	8 11
22 17	22 17	25 21	25 21	22 17
Refer to F-3	F-3	F-3	F-3	F-3

---

9 14	12 16	12 16	11 16	11 16
22 17	22 17	21 17	22 17	22 17
11 16	8 12	8 12	9 14	16 20
17 13	17 13	25 21	25 22	25 22
16 20	16 20	9 14	8 11	12 16
25 22	25 22	17 13	17 13	17 13
8 11	9 14	16 20	16 20	8 12
22 17	22 17	22 17	22 17	22 17
Refer to F-3	F-3	F-3	F-3	F-3

---

11 16	11 16	11 16	9 13	10 15
21 17	22 17	21 17	21 17	22 17
8 11	8 11	9 13	12 16	11 16
Refer to F-3	25 22	24 20	24 20	23 18
	F-4	F-5	F-5	F-6

11 15	11 15	10 15	10 14	9 14
22 17	24 20	24 20	22 17	24 20
9 14	7 11	7 10	6 10	5 9
25 22	28 24	28 24	17 13	22 17
15 19	3 7	3 7	1 6	1 5
Refer			24 20	17 13
to			11 15	11 15
F-7	F-8	F-8	F-9	F-9

---

11 15	10 14	10 14	9 14	9 14
22 18	24 20	22 18	24 20	22 18
15 22	11 15	6 10	6 9	6 9
25 18	22 18	24 20	22 18	24 20
10 14	15 22			
24 20	25 18			
6 10	6 10			
Refer				
to				
F-9	F-9	F-10	F-10	F-10

GAMES

MASTER OPENING 1 — 12 16, 24 20

12 16	5 14	8 15	9 13	15 19
24 20A	24 19F	25 22	24 19	16 11
8 12B	*11 15	4 8	15 24	19 24
28 24C	20 11	31 27	28 19	11 8
9 14D	15 24	8 11	11 15	H24 27
22 18E	27 20	27 24	19 16	DRAWN
3 8	*7 16	6 9	12 19	Wyllie v.
18 9	20 11	32 28	23 16	Yates

A. Known to book-players as the Dundee. An opening very favorable to White, who obtains a cramp on the Black single corner from the opening formation. It is, however, a sound draw when understood.

B. Affords support to the piece on 16 and prepares for an exchange by 16 19 as opportunity arises, relieving the cramped hold White obtained from the opening. 11 15 at once gives White the advantage.

C. Strongest, increasing the pressure and preventing Black from breaking the bonds for a time.

D. Best and most conservative. *Checker Classics* predicted history for 3 8, almost a year

43

prior to the Stewart-Banks Match. It was played in that match, but is hardly advisable for the student. 4 8 loses, but our text steers White into definite lines of analyzed play.

E. 22 17 is another popular variation: 22 17, 3 8, 26 22, 11 15, 20 11, 7 16, 24 20, 5 9**G**, 20 11, 15 18, 22 15, 10 26, 30 23, 8 15, 17 10, 15 19, 23 16, 12 19, 10 7, 2 11, 25 22, 11 15, 31 26, 4 8, DRAWN.—W. Gardner.

F. Forces 11 15 to maintain an equal position. 23 19 leads to play known as the Boston Cross, and is drawable.

G. 16 19 draws, but the cute little win for White if Black plays 15 19 is now history, and may be instructive to the student.

It is of interest to note, in presenting this position to the student, that Mr. J. P. Reed, who lost it, was a very prominent player of no mean ability, having drawn and scored games with practically all the well-known experts of his day, and if memory serves us correctly was champion of Pennsylvania for some years.

Mr. C. F. Barker, who won the game, was world champion for some years and the composer of many renowned problems, the majority of which he drew from his cross-board encounters with other well-known experts.

Black—1, 2, 4, 5, 6, 8, 10, 12, 14, 16, 19

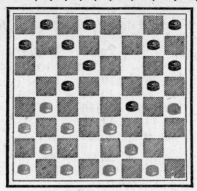

White—17, 20, 21, 22, 23, 25, 27, 29, 30, 31, 32

White to play and win

20 11, 8 15, 23 16, 12 19, 17 13, 5 9, 30 26,
4 8, 27 23, 19 24, 31 27, 24 31, 22 17, WHITE
WINS.—J. P. Reed *v.* C. F. Barker.

H. J. Lees, in his Guide tells us this opening received its name from Mr. A. J. Dunlap, who was Draughts Editor of the *New York Turf, Field and Farm*, in compliment to the members of the Dundee Draughts Club for an interesting analysis of the opening which they published in the Dundee *Weekly News*, early in the sixties.

Major Variation 1-A — 12 16, 23 19

The most dangerous of the Barred Openings, with the draw for White after the second move, still in doubt. The following collation of play may have concealed in it the necessary play to construct a sound draw for the White side.

Trunk

12 16	8 11	8 12⁶	10 19	15 18
23 19	30 26	19 16	17 10	24 15
16 23	4 8⁴	12 19	6 15	18 22
27 18	22 17⁵	23 16	27 24	
11 16	9 14	11 15	20 27	BLACK
26 23¹	18 9	25 22	31 24	WINS
16 20²	5 14	15 18	1 5	Reynolds
32 27³	24 19	22 15	21 17	v. J. Horr

Variation 1

22 17⁷	22 15	29 25	19 16	18 9
8 11⁸	20 27	2 7	10 19	5 21
17 14⁹	32 23	23 18	16 12	7 14
10 17	7 16	5 9	7 10	21 25
21 14	28 24	30 26	12 3	22 18
11 15	16 20	9 13	6 9	
18 11	25 22	24 19	21 17	
9 18	20 27	7 10	1 5	
26 22	31 24	25 21	3 7	DRAWN
16 20	4 8	3 7	9 14	Banks

Variation 2

8· 12	22 18	10 17	23 14	21 25
30 26	14 17	24 20	17 21	29 22
4 8	21 14	8 11	28 24	7 10
32 27	10 17	18 15	3 7	14 7
9 14	25 21	11 18	26 23	2 25
18 9	6 10	20 11	16 19	DRAWN
5 14	21 14	7 16	24 15	Hanson

Thus far it appears that 16 20 at seventh move
for Black is necessary to further the attack, and
that if a draw for White which will stand the test
is found it must be later in the game.

Variation 3

24 19	6 22	18 14	27 31	20 16
8 11	26 17	10 15	8 11	27 23
22 17 **10**	11 15	14 9	22 17	16 20
9 14	19 16	15 18	9 6	31 27
18 9	2 6	22 8	23 26	28 24
5 14	29 25	13 31	6 2	23 18
25 22	6 9	21 17	17 13	24 19
11 15 **11**	25 22 **13**	31 26	2 6	18 15
30 26 **A**	9 13	17 14	26 30	19 16
15 24	23 18	26 22	11 16	15 19
28 19	15 19	14 10	30 26	16 11
4 8	31 26	19 23	32 28	19 15
22 18 **12**	20 24	8 4	31 27	B. WINS
8 11	16 12	24 27	16 20	J. Horr *v.*
18 9	7 11	4 8	26 31	Reynolds

A. 30 25, 15 24, 28 19, 7 11, 17 13, 11 15,
32 28, 15 24, 28 19, 20 24, 22 18, 24 28, BLACK
WINS.—Published Play.

Variation 4

10 14	25 22	6 10	31 22	8 11
18 15 **B**	9 13	23 16	6 10	
11 18	29 25	1 6	22 18	
22 15	2 7	26 23	10 14	BLACK
4 8	19 16	14 18	18 9	WINS
24 19	10 19	23 14	5 14	Bradford
7 10	16 12	10 26	25 22	*v.* Lawson

B. Mr. Lawson might have drawn, with very careful play, by the following: 22 17, 4 8, 17 10, 7 14, 25 22, 8 12, 29 25, and now the formation is "a single corner position permitting of a critical draw."—P. H. Ketchum.

Variation 5

18 14[4]	8 11	22 18	14 17	17 10
9 18	26 23	10 14	25 22	13 17
23 14[5]	6 10	18 9	10 14	10 6
10 17	31 26	5 14	13 9	21 25
21 14[6]	10 17	29 25	17 21	6 2
11 15	22 13	7 10	9 6	25 30
24 19[7]	1 6c	19 16	2 9	B. WINS
15 24	25 22	11 15	22 17	J. Horr v.
28 19	6 10	16 12	9 15	Townsend

C. 5 9 also wins.—P. H. Ketchum.

Variation 6

11 15	7 11	8 11	11 15	20 27
25 22D, E	19 16F	22 18	26 17	31 24
15 24	11 15	15 22	2 7	B. WINS
28 19	16 12G	17 13	27 24	Howe, Jr.

D. 26 22, 15 24, 28 19, 8 11, 22 18, 1 5, 18 9, 5 14, 19 16, 11 15, 27 24, BLACK WINS.—Published Play.

E. 19 16, 8 12, 25 22, 12 19, 23 16, 15 18, 22 15, 10 19, 17 10, 6 15, and BLACK WINS.— Peter Doran.

F. 22 18, 8 12, 18 9, 6 22, 26 17, 11 15, 27 24,

20 27, 31 24, *1 5, 29 25, 5 9, 17 13, 3 8, and BLACK WINS.—John Howe, Jr.

G. 16 11, 8 12, 22 18, 15 22, 11 8, 12 16, 8 4, 10 15, 17 10, 15 19, BLACK WINS.—John Howe, Jr.

Variation 7

31 27	8	5 9	25 22	6 15	26 23
16 20	29 25H	5 9	19 10	21 25
24 19	9 13	21 17	9 14	18 14
8 12	22 18	11 16	18 9	25 30
18 14	7 11	28 24	11 15	9 6
9 18	26 23	7 11	23 18	3 8
22 15	1 5	17 14	8 11	BLACK
4 8	30 26	10 17	32 28	WINS
25 22	2 7	15 10	17 21	J. H. Scott

H. 22 18, 7 11, 29 25, 1 5, BLACK WINS.

Variation 8

16 20*19	31 27|21	9 13	25 21	19 26
17 14	20	4 8	24 19	2 7	30 23
10 17	25 22	6 9	21 14	7 10
21 14	8 12	19 15	16 19	
20 27	29 25	7 10	23 16	BLACK
32 23	11 16	15 6	12 19	WINS
8 11	28 24|22	1 17	26 23|1	J. Horr

I. If 30 25, 3 8, BLACK WINS.—J. F. Horr.

Variation 9

25 22	17 13	29 25	30 25	32 28
16 20	11 15	8 11	20 24	24 27
24 19	22 17	25 22	16 12	31 24
9 14	15 24	11 15	18 23	11 16
18 9	28 19	19 16	26 19	B. WINS
5 14	4 8	14 18	7 11	Lieberman

4

Variation 10

30 26	7 14	25 22	11 16	18 15
4 8	18 15**24**	14 18	27 23	10 14
32 27	11 18	23 14	5 9	28 24
10 14**J**	26 22	9 25	31 27	14 18
22 17**23**	3 8	29 22	6 10	BLACK
8 12	22 15	7 11	15 6	WINS
17 10	2 7	22 18	1 10	A. Jordan

J. 9 14, 18 9, 5 14, 22 18, 14 17, 21 14, 10 17, 25 21, 6 10, 21 14, 10 17, 26 22, DRAWN.—Published Play.

Variation 11

4 8	32 27	10 19	31 24**M**	18 22
30 26**K**	12 19	17 10	1 5	
11 15	23 16	6 15	21 17	BLACK
19 16	15 18**L**	27 24	15 18	WINS
8 12	22 15	20 27	24 15	Reynolds

K. 22 18 was played at this point in the Fourth American Tourney, but later analysis will detect the weak point.

L. Improves Kear's Encyclopedia, where 7 11 allows a draw.

M. A pretty win.

Variation 12

32 27	26 17	17 10	27 24	21 17
8 11**25**	11 15	7 14	20 27	14 21
22 18	19 16	29 25	31 24	23 18
1 5	5 9	9 13	7 10	15 19
18 9	16 12**26**	25 22	24 20	B. WINS
6 22	10 14	2 7	3 7	Banks

Variation 13

17	1327	31	22	18	15	9	6	4	8
9	14	7	11	*20	24o	26	22	24	27
16	1228	13	9	17	14	6	2	8	11
14	17	11	16	23	2629	16	19	27	31
21	14	23	18	14	10	11	8	11	16
10	17	15	19	26	30	22	17	B. WINS	
25	22	22	17N	15	11	8	4	Roberts v.	
17	26	19	23	30	26	19	23	Broadbent	

N. 18 15, 19 23, 15 10, 20 24, BLACK WINS.—
J. Howe, Jr.

O. Best, as 23 26 may allow a draw.

Variation 14

18 15P	10 19	24 15	11 18	Q22 15

P. If 24 19, 10 14, the position is same as
Variation 9 at fourth move.

Q. The position is now a problem, Black to
play and win.

For the benefit of those students to whom the
name of Alexander (the gentleman accredited
with the play for the win) is little more than a
name, we take pleasure in stating that Mr.
Alexander is a very noted English player of
some years standing. He is known chiefly as
the collaborator of Kear's Encyclopedia, but is
also recognized as one of the foremost analysts
of Great Britain and is the author of many
articles pertaining to the pastime both here and
abroad.

White—15, 21, 23, 25, 26, 27, 28, 29, 31

Black—1, 2, 3, 5, 6, 7, 8, 9, 20

Black to play and win

*7 10, 25 22, 10 19, 23 16, ***6 10, 22 1830,**
2 7, 29 25, 9 13, 16 1231, 8 11, 26 23ʀ, ***5 9,**
18 14s, 9 18, 23 14, 10 17, 21 14, BLACK WINS.—
Alexander.

R. 18 14, 10 17, 21 14, **13 17,** 25 22, **17 21,**
26 23, 21 25, 23 19, 25 30, 22 18, 30 25, 27 23,
BLACK WINS.—Trigg.

S. 25 22, 10 14, 27 24, 20 27, 31 24, 11 16,
24 20, 7 11, 28 24, 1 6, BLACK WINS.—P. Doran
v. Howe, Jr.

A few years ago Messrs. Doran and Howe
collaborated in compiling quite a searching
analysis bearing on this opening.

Variation 15

22	15	6	9	27	23	5	14	22	17
10	19**32**	26	23	6	9	31	22	30	26
24	15	9	18	14	10	16	19	2	6
11	18	23	14	9	14	13	9	26	22
23	14	7	11	17	13	19	23**U**	17	13
8	11	22	17	15	19	9	6	14	18
25	22	11	16	22	18	23	26	DRAWN	
11	15	25	22**T**	19	26	6	2	Howe, Jr.,	
29	25	2	6	18	9	26	30	*v.* Doran	

T. 17 13, 3 7, 21 17, 1 6, 31 26, 6 9, 13 6, 2 18, 26 23, 7 11, 23 14, 15 18, BLACK WINS.—P. Doran.

U. 20 24 also draws.—P. Doran.

Variation 16

22	13	8	11	31	26	9	18	10	7
11	15	29	25	1	5	13	9	11	15
26	23	11	15	22	17	5	14	7	2
5	9	18	11	14	18	17	10	16	19
23	18	7	16	26	23	3	8	BLACK	
15	22	25	22	6	9	21	17	WINS	
25	18	9	14	23	14	8	11	Fiedler	

Variation 17

22	17**33**	9	18	17	13	5	9	26	23
8	11	23	14	*7	10**34**	22	17	BLACK	
25	21	11	16	14	7	9	14	WINS	
6	9**V**	29	25	3	10	31	26	Doran *v.*	
26	23	2	6	25	22	1	5	Howe, Jr.	

V. Improves Kear's, where 15 18 is given, and 29 25 in reply is starred to draw.

Variation 18

32 27	7 10	31 15	5 14	22 17
16 20	22 18	3 7	28 24	8 12
18 15	10 19	25 22	7 10	26 23
10 19	27 24	9 14	24 19	B. WINS
24 15	20 27	18 9	2 7	Ketchum

Variation 19

9 14	6 9	16 23	27 24	3 7
18 9	25 22	26 19	22 17	22 18
5 14	2 6	10 14	24 19	7 10
25 22	17 13	19 15	30 25	17 14
16 20	4 8	14 23	12 16	10 19
22 18	28 24	15 8	25 22	14 5
14 23	8 12	23 27	19 24	23 26
26 19	*31 26	8 4	11 15	20 16
20 27	11 16	27 31	16 19	
32 23	24 20	4 8	15 11	DRAWN
8 11	7 11	31 27	19 23	Howe, Jr.,
29 25	23 18	8 11	11 15	*v.* Doran

Variation 20

24 19	28 19	14 7	12 8	22 17
9 14	7 11 35	3 10 36	24 19	8 3
18 9	*22 18	29 25	8 3	17 10
5 14	8 12	24 28	19 15	9 13
25 22	18 9	31 26	3 8	23 18
8 11	6 22	28 32	10 14	2 7
26 23	26 17	20 16	26 23	18 14
4 8	20 24	12 19	1 5	13 17
30 26	27 20	23 16	25 22	10 6
11 15	11 15	32 27	5 9	BLACK
32 27	17 14	16 12	8 11	WINS
15 24	15 24	27 24	15 8	Tescheleit

Variation 21

23	19	9	13 38	30	26	6	9	23 14
4	8	25	21	2	6	18	15	3 8
26	23 37	*13	17 39	20	16	9	18	B. WINS
8	12	24	20	11	20	15	6	Howe, Jr.,
28	24	6	10	31	27	1	10	v. Doran

Variation 22

25	21	3	8	26	22	23	26	28 24
9	13	9	5	11	18	11	7	22 29
14	9	2	7	22	15	26	30	10 6
5	14	27	24	14	18	7	2	1 10
18	9	16	19	24	20	6	9	7 23
7	10 40	23	16	19	23	2	7	13 17
22	18	12	19	20	16	30	26	21 14
10	14	30	25	8	12	15	10	B. WINS
18	15	7	11	16	11	26	22	Banks

Variation 23

18	15 W	29	25	23	16	31	22	BLACK
11	18	2	7	1	6	6	10	WINS
22	15	19	16	26	23	22	18	Bradford
7	10 X	10	19	14	18	10	14	v. Lawson
25	22	16	12	23	14	18	9	Fourth
9	13	6	10	10	26	5	14	A.T., 1920

W. Equally fatal is 19 15, as follows:

19	15	9	13	31	24	*13	17	B. WINS
20	24	18	9	5	14	22	13	Doran v.
27	20	11	27	26	23	6	10	Howe, Jr.

X. The following fine play also wins for Black:

7	11	22	15	9	13 Y	19	16	6	10
26	22	2	7	31	26	12	19	B. WINS
11	18	25	22	8	12	23	16	Pub. Play

Y.   14 18, 23 14, 9 25, 29 22, 5 9, 22 18z, 7 10, 31 26A, 3 7, 21 17, 8 12, 17 13, 10 14, 27 23, 7 10, BLACK WINS.—J. Duffy.

Z.   19 16, 9 14, 22 17, 14 18, 16 12, 18 22, BLACK WINS.

A.   21 17, 9 13, 18 14, 13 22, 14 7, 3 10, 19 16, 10 19, 16 12, 19 23, BLACK WINS.

Variation 24

26 22	2 9	7 2	23 26	9 13	
11 16	23 14	9 13	2 6	31 27	
22 17	16 32	28 24	26 30	13 22	
6 10	14 10	12 16	11 7	1 6	
17 13	32 27	24 20	13 17		
10 15B	31 24	16 19	21 14	BLACK	
18 11	20 27	20 16	30 21	WINS	
14 18	11 7	19 23	6 9	Hugh	
13 6	27 31	16 11	21 17	Henderson	

B.   3 7, BLACK WINS.—Published Play.

Variation 25

7 11	27 20	24 28	17 14	18 14	
22 18	11 15	18 14	24 19	2 7	
8 12	17 14	28 32	14 9	14 9	
18 9	15 24	14 10	19 15	7 16	
6 22	14 7	32 28	9 6	12 19	
26 17	2 11	21 17	15 18	B. WINS	
20 24*	23 18 41	28 24	6 2	Moore	

Variation 26

17 13	25 22	26 19	16 7	11 7
2 6	14 17	17 26	3 10	23 16
29 25	21 14	18 1542	15 11	7 2
9 14	10 17	26 31	31 27	16 11
31 26	23 18	27 23	23 18	B. WINS
15 19	19 23	7 11	27 23	J. Jack

Variation 27

16 12	23 18	17 14	23 18	10 6
9 13	15 19	24 28	19 23	1 10
25 22	18 14	14 9	9 6	2 6
7 11	10 15	28 32	23 26	32 28
32 27	14 10	27 23	6 2	B. WINS
11 16	19 24	15 19	26 30	P. Doran

Variation 28

13 9	32 28	31 26	23 16	24 20
14 17	17 21	20 24	27 31	25 30
21 14	25 22	16 12	28 24	B. WINS
10 17	15 19c	24 27	21 25	J. Horr

C. 21 25 only draws, as played by Horr *v.* Long.

Variation 29

24 27	6 2	20 24	11 7	18 22
14 10	26 23	28 19	20 24	6 2
27 31	11 8	23 16	6 2	22 17
15 11	27 31	8 11	24 19	2 6
31 26	8 4	16 20	2 6	17 13
32 28	31 26	7 2	19 23	6 2
16 20	4 8	22 17	6 2	13 9
9 6	26 22	2 6	23 18	B. WINS
23 7	2 7	17 14	2 6	Howe, Jr.

Variation 30

28 24	20 27	16 7	14 21	17 13
2 7D	31 24	10 14	11 7	18 22
24 19	9 14	18 11	5 9	13 9
8 11 43	21 17	3 10	7 2	1 10
26 23	14 21	22 17	10 14	DRAWN
11 15 E	23 18	21 25	22 17	Horr v.
27 24	7 11	29 22	14 18	Long

D. C. Nelson and J. F. Horr have both expressed the belief that 8 12 might on analysis show a win here.

E. The following was contested some years back:

9 13	21 14	17 22	27 23	5 14
22 18	10 17	23 18	6 10	18 9
13 17	18 14	1 6	14 9	DRAWN

J. H. Scott v. Newell W. Banks

Variation 31

28 24	7 10	23 19	21 25	22 18
8 11	27 23	11 16	10 7	20 24
25 22	20 27	19 10	3 10	6 2
10 15	31 24	16 20	15 6	24 27
21 17	1 5	24 19	25 30	2 7
5 9	17 14	17 21	26 23	B. WINS
16 12	10 17	18 15	30 26	Ketchum

Variation 32

11 18	10 17	6 9	9 18	2 6
23 14	21 14	26 23	23 14	25 22

Variation 32—*continued*

6 10	26 23	9 18	27 18	7 10
22 17	15 19	24 19	20 27	11 7
1 6	23 16	8 12	18 15	31 27
31 26	6 9	28 24	27 31	B. WINS
10 15	29 25	18 23	15 11	Ketchum

Variation 33

25 21	27 23	19 15	15 11	6 2
8 11F	7 14	9 13	31 27	9 14
29 25	23 16	26 22H	11 7	14 17
11 16	20 27	18 23	27 23	21 14
22 17	31 24	22 18	7 2	18 9
16 19	5 9	6 9	23 19I	7 2
14 10G	24 19	15 10	16 12J	13 17
7 14	15 24	23 26	19 15	BLACK
17 10	28 19	18 15	2 6	WINS
2 7	14 18	26 31	15 18	J. H. Scott

F. 6 9 permits a draw. Jordan *v.* Banks.

G. 25 22, 6 10, 27 23, 20 27, 31 24, 15 18, 22 6, 2 27, 24 15, 27 31, BLACK WINS.

H. If 15 11 or 16 11, then 18 22, 25 18, 3 7, and BLACK WINS by First Position.—P. H. Ketchum.

I. *23 18, 16 12K, 9 14, 2 7, 14 17, 21 14, 18 9, 13 17, 25 21, 17 22, 21 17, 22 26, BLACK WINS.—Scott.

J. 2 7, 19 12, 7 11, DRAWN.—J. Duffy.

K. 2 6, 9 14, 6 9. 13 17, BLACK WINS.

Variation 34

16 19	25 22	10 19	15 11	25 21
21 17ʟ	5 9	27 24	25 30	17 14
7 10	22 18	20 27	11 7	9 18
14 7	15 22	31 15	30 25	B. WINS
3 10	24 15	22 25	7 2	Kear, Jr.

L. The following improvement on Kear's has been noted:

31 26, 13 6, 21 14, 14 7, 25 21, 6 9, 1 17, 7 10, 3 10, 10 14ᴍ.

M. Left here as a black win by **Kear, Jr.** The continuing play is by Mr. Clark:

Black—5, 14, 15, 19, 20

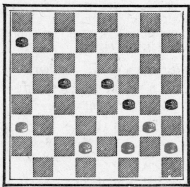

White—21, 24, 26, 27, 28

White to play and draw

27 23	5 9	26 22	27 31	2 6
20 27	16 11	9 13	7 2	DRAWN
23 16	15 19	11 7	31 26	J. W. Clark

Variation 35

8	11	19	16	5	9	23	18	31	27
22	18	15	19	13	6	7	11	6	1
1	5	29	25	2	9	18	14	27	23
18	9	19	26	16	12	24	27	1	5
6	22	31	22	*9	1344	14	10	B. WINS
26	17	10	15	27	23	27	31	Cronk v.
11	15	17	13	20	24	10	6	W. Dixon

Variation 36

2	11	22	18	19	15	10	7	17	22
21	17	28	24	26	22	14	21	10	14
24	28	*14	10	15	19	7	3	22	26
17	14	7	14	22	17	16	19	14	10
3	7	18	9	19	15	3	7	26	30
29	25	12	16	18	14	11	15	20	16
28	32	23	18	15	18	7	10	BLACK
25	22	24	19	14	10	21	17	WINS
32	28	*31	26	18	14	9	5	Dixon

Variation 37

25	22	16	20	22	17	7	11	5	9
8	12	28	24	9	13	9	5	14	18
29	2545	3	7	26	22	6	9	23	7
11	16	30	26	1	6	5	1	16	32
26	23	11	16	14	9	11	15	BLACK
7	11	25	21	5	14	1	5	WINS
31	27	6	10	18	9	9	14	Smith

Variation 38

11	16	9	13	7	16	3	746	5	14
24	20	20	11	25	22	14	947	18	9

Variation 38—*continued*

16	20	9	5	16	20	23	16	2 9
30	26	11	16	29	25	27	31	16 11
20	24	18	15	20	27	25	22	BLACK
22	18	24	27	19	16	6	10	WINS
7	11	31	24	12	19	15	6	Broadbent

Variation 39

11	15	*31	27	6	15	30	23	31 26
18	11	13	17	18	11	19	26	29 25
7	16	19	15	*1	6	4	8	20 24
24	20	17	22	11	8	16	20	
3	7	23	18	12	16	27	23	
20	11	16	19	8	4	26	31	DRAWN
7	16	15	10	22	26	23	19	Banks

Variation 40

16	19	16	11	*2	7	24	20	26 31
23	16	7	16	30	26	17	22	8 4
12	19	22	18	7	11	19	16	31 26
27	23N	14	23	26	23	11	15	4 8
1	5	26	12	10	14	16	11	26 22
23	16	6	10	23	19	22	26	B. WINS
5	14	28	24	13	17	11	8	M-S. C.

N.   9 5,   3 8,   22 18,   8 12,   18 15,   DRAWN.—
Banks.

Variation 41

21	17	3	7	25	2248	28	24	18 19
24	28	29	25	32	28	14	100	Pos.
17	14	28	32	22	18	7	14	

O.   31 26, 1 6, 26 22, 6 10, 14 9, 10 14, B. WINS.

Position.—The position at this point forms a pretty problem:

White—9, 20, 23, 31

Black—1, 11, 12, K-24

Black to play and win

12 16	19 15	19 15	18 14	16 19
23 18	26 22	18 14	10 7	3 8
24 19	15 19	15 18	14 21	B. WINS
31 26	22 17	14 10	7 3	Ketchum

Variation 42

27 23	7 10	15 11	24 28	19 15
26 31	23 19	14 17	4 8	23 18
16 12	27 23	11 8	28 32	BLACK
31 27	18 15	20 24	8 11	WINS
19 16	10 14	8 4	32 28	J. Jack

Variation 43

8	12*	22 18	12 26	27 23	24 27
26	23 49	5 9	22 15	30 26	11 7
9	14	18 15Q	1 5	23 19	27 31
31	26P	11 18	3 7	26 17	7 2
3	8	26 22R	26 30	7 10	31 26
29	25	10 15	25 22	20 24	B. WINS
8	11	19 3	9 13	15 11	Dougherty

P.   22 17, 10 15, 19 10, 12 26, 31 22, 7 11, 17 13, 11 15, 13 9, 15 19, 29 25, 19 24, 27 23, 24 27, BLACK WINS.

Q.   26 22, 9 13, 18 9, 11 15, BLACK WINS.

R.   16 11, 7 16, 26 22, 1 5, 22 6, 14 17, B. WINS.

Variation 44

15 19	27 31	10 14	27 31	20 16
21 17	14 9	25 21	1 5	9 18
9 13	31 27	23 19	31 27	16 7
17 14	9 6	16 11	5 1	22 17
19 24	27 23	20 24	27 24	13 22
27 23	19 16	1 5	1 5	18 25
24 27	7 10	24 27	24 20	DRAWN
23 19	*6 1	5 1	5 9	Dixon

Variation 45

19 15	16 20	22 17	5 9	23 18
11 16	29 25	9 13	14 5	25 30
15 11	7 11	26 22	6 9	18 14
16 19	31 27	7 11	17 14	30 26
11 8	2 7	27 23	11 15	14 10
12 16	25 21	19 26	18 11	B. WINS
8 4	11 16	30 23	9 25	Ketchum

Variation 46

6 9*50	30 26	12 16	11 2	25 30
29 25	16 20	21 17	10 15	26 22
2 7	31 27s	8 12	18 11	30 26
25 215ı	3 8	15 11	9 25	B. WINS
1 6	19 15	6 10	17 14	Tanner

S.   22 17, 13 22, 26 17, 20 24, 17 13, 24 28, and BLACK WINS.—Published Play.

Variation 47

30 26	15 10	3 8	17 14	8 4
6 10	7 11	20 24	28 32	18 9
29 25	10 7	8 11	11 16	4 8
10 17	11 16	32 28	32 27	13 17
25 21	7 3	23 19	15 11	24 20
16 20	28 32	1 6	27 23	17 22
21 14	22 17	18 15	11 8	16 11
20 24	13 22	6 9	24 27	9 14
19 15	26 17	14 10	31 24	DRAWN
24 28	16 20	9 13	23 18	J. H. Finn

Variation 48

25 21	26 22	21 17	14 9
32 28	24 27	1 6	10 15	BLACK
31 26	22 18	17 13	18 14	WINS
28 24	27 24	6 10	15 18	Ketchum

Variation 49

29 25т	17 13	9 6	14 5	17 14
9 14	19 24	14 18	7 14	19 16
22 17	13 9	23 14	25 22	14 10
10 15	24 28	32 23	23 19	16 11
19 10	26 23	6 2	22 17	B. WINS
12 19	28 32	5 9	14 18	Ketchum
5				

T.   22 18, 9 14, 18 9, 5 14, 26 23, 3 8, 29 25,
8 11, 25 22, 11 15, 27 24, 20 27, 31 24, 14 18,
and BLACK WINS.—P. H. Ketchum.

Variation 50

16 20U	23 14	7 11	30 23	13 22
31 27	1 6	10 7	12 16	6 13
6 9	25 21	11 16	7 2	27 31
29 25	6 9	19 15	20 24	14 9
2 7	22 18	16 19	22 6	DRAWN
18 15	3 8	27 23	24 27	Tescheleit
9 18	15 10	19 26	21 17 v.	S. Cohen

U.   6 9 as in Variation 46 is correct to win.
This was one of the concluding games in the 1924
English Tourney.

Variation 51

31 27	10 26	23 18	14 17	6 9
1 6	20 2	27 23	25 22	14 17
27 24	26 31	15 11	17 26	9 14
6 10	18 15	23 14	30 23	B. WINS
24 20	31 27	2 6	9 14	Smith

Major Variation 1-B — 12 16, 22 17

12 16	6 9D	9 18	9 18	7 10
22 17	23 14	31 26	17 14	14 7
16 19A	9 18	8 11	10 17	3 10
24 15	30 26	26 23	21 14	22 17
11 18B	1 6	2 6	11 15	F15 18
23 14	26 23	23 14	25 22E	DRAWN
9 18	6 9	6 9	18 25	Long v.
26 23C	23 14	28 24	29 22	Tanner

A. It is becoming a difficult question to answer as to just what it is best for Black to play here. Some players in high favor have begun to discard the 16 19, due to the after strength of the White game, opposed to which is the fact that White makes Black feel the pressure if 16 20 is taken: 16 20, 17 14, 10 17, 21 14, 9 18, 23 14, 6 9N, 26 23, 9 18, 23 14, 1 6, 30 26, 6 9, 26 23, 9 18, 23 14, 2 6, 24 19, 6 9, 31 26, 9 18, 19 15, etc., DRAWN, a line in which Black has shouldered all the hard work.

N. If 11 15, 24 19, 15 24, 28 19, and White secures a powerful game containing winning chances.

B. 10 19, 23 16, 11 20 is falling into disuse, probably due to Black's unaggressive formation. There are various continuations which are eventually drawn. Mr. Banks is credited with introducing the 11 18 take.

C. The accepted move and most preferred, weakening Black's double corner.

D. 10 14 is not a likely move, creating, as it does, a source of danger for the piece on 18 and discounting the effect on square 19.

E. The usual and safe way to play the game. The continual manning-off has finally resulted in a clean-cut draw.

F. The foregoing game is from the Fifth American Tourney, and it may be of interest to note that it is almost a duplicate of the play between Messrs. Stewart and Banks in their championship tilt, played in Scotland in 1922, a few months previous.

Major Variation 1-C — 12 16, 21 17

12 16	10 17	6 10	13 22	I11 15
21 17	21 14	30 25	26 17D	24 20
9 13A	6 10	10 17	8 11	15 24
25 21B	29 25	25 21	24 19	28 19
16 19	10 17	2 6	4 8E	8 11
23 16	25 21	21 14	27 24F	DRAWN
11 20	1 6	6 10	20 27	Ferrie v.
17 14C	21 14	22 17	31 24	Jordan

A. Best, though 16 19 and 16 20 are also playable.

B. 24 20 leads to a complicated game by 11 15, 20 11, 7 16, etc., and gives Black a slightly superior position.

C. 29 25 also draws: 29 25, 5 9, 17 14, 9 18, 22 15, 10 19, 24 15, 7 10, 27 23, 10 19, 23 16, 8 12, 32 27, 12 19, 27 24, 20 27, 31 15, 13 17, 21 14, 6 10, 15 6, 2 18, 28 24, 4 8, 25 22, 18 25, 30 21, 8 11, 24 19, 1 6, 26 23, 6 10, 23 18, 3 8, DRAWN.—Jordan v. Gall.

D. The attack on Black's double corner has now been successfully defended, and the position on both sides is at least equal. The line given is perhaps the easiest one for study by the student, in an opening considered a dangerous one for both sides.

E. 11 15, 27 23, 15 24, 28 19, 4 8, 23 18, 8 11, then 31 27 draws by 10 15, 19 10, 5 9, 14 5, 7 21, 18 15, 11 18, 27 24, 20 27, 32 14; or if instead of 31 27, a sound draw is obtained by 32 28 with either 20 24 or 10 15 in reply. A Jordan-Banks ending, varied at sixth move of this note with 32 27 to a drawn result.

F. This is best, allowing White 24 20 if 11 15 is made in reply. 27 23, 8 12, 23 18**G**, 12 16, 19 12, 10 15, and BLACK WINS. Banks *v.* J. Horr. Second American Tourney.

G. 31 26, 20 24**H**, 19 16, 12 19, 23 16, 11 20, 28 19, DRAWN.—A. Jordan.

H. 11 15, 26 22, 15 24, 28 19, 10 15, DRAWN. —A. Jordan.

I. Black has nothing better, the two for two would be dangerous, allowing White to get a quick king at his rear.

First Position

By William Payne

This is without doubt one of the most important end-game positions in the study of Checkers. It will be frequently encountered in cross-board play. The method of forcing the win distinctly demonstrates the science of the game, and should be memorized by every student.

Black 12, King 28

White Kings 23, 27

White to play and win

27 32	28 24	28 32	16 19	11 15
28 24	32 28	27 24	32 27	32 28
23 18	24 27	18 15	28 32	15 19
24 28A	15 18	24 28	27 31	WHITE
18 15	12 16	*15 11	19 23	WINS

A

12 16	32 28	11 8	27 23
18 15	19 16	28 32	8 3
16 20	18 23	8 11	23 18
15 18	16 11	32 27	3 8
24 19	23 19	11 8	18 15 WHITE WINS

11 16	5 14	4 8	11 27	19 23
24 20A	25 22	25 22	32 14	26 19
16 19	10 15C	2 6	1 5	11 16
23 16	22 17	22 17	31 27	25 22
12 19	6 10	8 12	3 8F	16 23
22 18	29 25	27 24E	*30 25G	DRAWN
9 14B	8 11D	14 18	8 11	Schmutz *v*.
18 9	17 13	20 16	*27 24G	Reynolds

A. The Bristol opening. An entertaining game equal in scope with 11 15. Many brilliant positions arise from it.

B. Conservative, but best, Black now having command of both key squares. There is much play arising from 10 14, leading to very intricate positions not advisable for practice by the student.

C. Practically all of the older textbooks on the game exhausted their fund of adjectives in describing this move as "safe," "sound," etc., but failed to exhaust themselves in giving play upon it. Taken up some years ago, for that very reason by the experts, it is now the most popular continuation for Black.

D. Standard play, and best. Dougherty moved 8 12 against Horr in the Fourth American Tourney, and the subsequent play ran:

8 12	10 14	8 11	14 17	6 10
17 13	17 10	24 20	21 14	27 24
4 8	7 14	2 6	18 23	10 17
25 22	20 16	32 27	27 18	24 8
14 18	3 7	1 5	15 29	12 19
22 17	27 24	30 25	31 27	DRAWN

E. 27 23, 3 8, 23 16, 12 19, 26 23, 19 26, 30 23, 8 12, 32 27N, 1 5, 27 24, *14 18, 23 14, 12 16, BLACK WINS.—Published Play.

N. 28 24, 15 18, 24 19, 18 27, 31 24, 11 15, 20 16, 15 18, 24 20, 18 22, 19 15, etc., DRAWN.—Scott v. Weslow.

F. An improvement originated and introduced by Mr. A. P. Schmutz of Philadelphia in correspondence with W. B. Hart of Harrisburg, Pa. It introduces a new and tricky line of play, improving upon the usual 12 16.

G. In the above mentioned correspondence game with Mr. Hart, these two starred moves were transposed, which is immaterial, providing they are both played following 3 8, and 8 11 on Black's part. The annotators of the Fifth American Tourney book failed to credit the originator in examining the Long-Townsend games.

Major Variation 2-A — 11 16, 24 19

11	16	7	10D	13	22	11	18	2	7
24	19A	30	26E	18	9	23	7	18	15
8	11	11	16	6	13	*3	10	10	19
22	18	26	22	25	18	25	22	27	24
10	14B	9	13	4	8	16	23	20	27
26	22	18	9	*29	25F	27	18	DRAWN	
16	20	5	14	8	11	1	5	Long v.	
22	17C	22	18	18	15G	32	27	Tanner	

A. The late Judge Janvier of Delaware bestowed the title of Paisley upon this opening formation, to distinguish it from other White replies to 11 16. We find it without doubt the best reply to 11 16 at White's command, forming an entertaining opening.

B. Preventing the 18 14 double exchange, aptly named, and well known as the "Paisley Bust."

C. While 30 26 is in itself sound, it affords Black an opportunity for a very clever trap by 4 8, 22 17, 11 16, 17 10, 6 24, 28 19, 7 10, etc., BLACK WINS.—Hugh Henderson. A full résumé of the necessary play to complete the win will be found in the Third American Tourney.

D. It would be premature and lead to bad results to make this move before 22 17 forces it. It is then best.

E. Mr. A. Jordan's predilection for 28 24 develops some tricky play against an unobservant opponent.   The Third American Tourney gives quite a sermon to the student against playing 11 16 before square 30 has been vacated.   Also drawable here, but slightly inferior is: 17 13, 3 7, 31 26, 12 16, 19 12, 4 8, 12 3, 14 17, 21 14, 10 17, 3 10, 6 31, 13 6, 31 24, 28 19, 1 10, 23 18, 10 14, 18 9, 5 14, 32 27, 2 6N, 19 16, 6 9, 16 7, 17 22, 25 18, 14 32, 29 25, 32 27, 25 22, 9 13, 22 18, 27 23, DRAWN.   Jordan v. Newcomb.

N.   Mr. Jordan considers this best, and makes White play carefully for the draw.

F.   18 15 loses by 1 6, 29 25, 3 7, 25 22, 7 11, 22 18, 2 7, 18 14, 10 17, 21 14, 11 18, 19 15, 13 17, 14 9, 6 13, BLACK WINS.—John Dougherty.

G.   The game has now arrived at a well-known position leading to a sound draw.   It has been played safely on well-known sound lines, and is the usual method of running it up, as played at the present time among the experts.   For this reason, we strongly urge its adoption by the student.

Major Variation 2-B — 11 16, 23 19

11 16	22 18D	6 9E	21 14	8 11
23 19A	4 8	24 20	10 17	32 27
16 23	18 9	15 24	26 22	3 7
26 19B	5 14	28 19	17 26	18 15
9 14C	25 22	9 13	31 22F	11 18
27 23	11 15	22 18	7 10	22 6
8 11	30 26	14 17	29 25	1 10

Major Variation 2-B—*continued*

*25	22G	18	15	20	11	24	20	8	3
10	14	17	22	22	25	30	26	DRAWN
22	18	15	11	27	24	11	8	Long *v.*
14	17	7	16	25	30	2	6	Horr

A. The second of the heretofore "Barred Openings," and, like the first (12 16, 23 19), although seeming hopeless for White at the beginning, no absolute Black wins have been discovered to date. Certain lines of the after-play have been shown to run into standard lines of the Defiance (Minor Variation 1, Opening 3) and the Laird & Lady Refused, another of the old-time openings.

B. The correct take, only advisable in this game, as in the other three "Barred Openings" 27 18 is best. If 27 18 is taken in the present case, followed by 12 16, we have 1-A at fifth move. For that reason in this game the 26 19 take is best, preventing a position counterpart with 1-A, which is conceded weaker for White.

C. Considered by the best players to be Black's wisest move here. This opinion is supported by an examination of published play.

D. Believed at one time to allow Black too great a choice of attacks, 22 17 being the move given with 11 15 in reply, leading to a drawn game. Mr. J. F. Horr improved published play by going 5 9 against 22 17, and as 5 9 seems to be the move, we advocate this 22 18 as best.

E. 8 11 is also good, as played by A. Jordan against J. F. Horr in the Fourth American Tourney to a drawn result.

F. This exchange seems to assure the draw, as following Black's next two moves, White plays 29 25 and 32 27 as given in the text, and obtains a powerful center.

G. Probably best. If 25 21, 13 17, 21 14, 10 17, then either 19 15, or 23 18, and Black plays 17 22, with the win in the ending.

Major Variation 2-C — 11 16, 22 17

11 16	8 11	9 14	7 10F	7 11
22 17	27 23c	18 9	30 26	17 13
16 19A	4 8D	6 22	9 14	11 15
24 15	23 16	26 17	26 23	27 24
10 19	11 20	11 15	3 7	20 27
23 16	22 18	29 25	23 19	G31 24
12 19	8 11E	5 9	15 24	DRAWN
25 22B	32 27	25 22	28 19	Various

A. The double exchange forms the Dyke, an opening formation slightly favoring Black, whose strength lies in establishing and maintaining a piece on key-square 19. The Transposition Tables show the position is now counterpart with 11 15, 22 17, 15 19, but 10 15 leads to 2-D.

B. 27 24, or 27 23, or 26 22, are also playable, but except 26 22 are not as strong as the text. Following this latter move, White continues with 30 26, making a transposition of

moves, arriving at the same position as if he had
played 25 22, and then 30 25. See Note **C**.

C. It is difficult in Checkers to say exactly
what is new and what is old. At any rate, this
is the move now in favor, though many still pre-
fer 30 25, which is equally as good if understood.

D. 11 16 is also quite good here. Its advantage if any lies in maintaining a piece on key-
square 19.

E. Older play here is 9 14, 18 9, 6 22, 26 17,
8 11, 29 25, 11 15, 25 22, 5 9, then if 32 27, same
as trunk at 24th move. If instead of 32 27 at
last move of this note, 30 26 be played, then 7 10,
26 23, 9 14, 23 19, 15 24, 28 19, 3 8, 19 15, 10 19,
17 10, 19 23, 22 18, 8 12, 18 15, 12 16, 15 11,
16 19, 32 28, 2 6, 10 7, 6 10, 7 2, DRAWN.—Alfred
Jordan.

F. If 7 11, 30 26, 11 16, 17 13, 9 14, 27 23,
and we have a pleasing position.

Mr. Willis G. Hill, the gentleman responsible
for the draw play on this position, is a resident
of Boston, Mass. He has participated in practically all the National Tourneys, with creditable
results and has made an enviable name for himself throughout the checker world as a careful
player and a worthy opponent. Mr. Hill also
has quite a reputation as a problem solver,
which, of course, is one of the secrets of his
remarkable skill at the game.

White—13, 21, 22, 23, 26, 28, 31

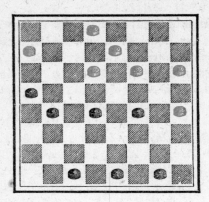

Black—1, 2, 3, 14, 15, 16, 20

Black to play and draw

15 19, 22 18, 1 5, 18 9, 5 14, 13 9, 3 8, 9 5, 8 12,
5 1, 14 18, 23 14, 19 24, 28 19, 16 30, DRAWN.—
Willis G. Hill *v.* J. H. Scott.

G. A run-up of play frequently met with
among present day experts, which we strongly
recommend to the student.

Major Variation 2-D — 11 16, 21 17

11 16	23 14	16 19	24 20	15 19
21 17	8 11	29 25	12 16	24 15
10 15A	22 17C	6 10	27 24	F11 25
17 14B	4 8D	25 22E	19 23	
9 18	25 21	1 6	26 12	

A. The Kelso, a formation which restricted Checkers has made as familiar as the older openings. Many beautiful positions arise from it.

B. A strong attack, occupying key-square 14, given by J. Alexander in Kear's Encyclopedia. Another good line is 22 18, 15 22, 25 18, 16 20, 17 13, 8 11, 29 25, 9 14, 18 9, 5 14, 24 19, 11 16, 19 15, 4 8, 23 19, 16 23, 27 9, 7 10, 25 22, 10 19, 22 18, 3 7, 32 27, 7 10, 9 5, 12 16, 13 9, 6 13, 27 24, DRAWN.—R. Jordan *v.* R. Stewart.

C. The Playing Charts and Transposition Tables show the formation is now counterpart with 10 15, 22 17, as well as 10 15, 21 17, thus enabling the student to use one line of play to cover three opening formations.

D. If 6 9, 26 23, 9 18, 23 14, then 1 6, or 16 20, followed by 25 21, etc., DRAWS.—Alexander, Jordan, etc.

E. To the student in search of "fireworks" and who is also anxious to cut down the number of pieces quickly we recommend the following: 17 13, 10 17, 21 14, 1 6, 24 20, 6 9, 13 6, 22 18, 26 23, 19 26, 30 14, 15 18, 27 23, 18 27, 32 23, 7 10, 14 7, 3 10, 25 22, 5 9, 23 19, etc., DRAWN.— J. Alexander and others.

F. To this point in our game the play is by Mr. J. Alexander, one of the finest of the English players and analysts, whose labors in Kear's

Encyclopedia will be appreciated for some time
to come.   Mr. Alexander leaves the play at this
point with the comment, "Black is best."   Our
continuation is from the Third American Tourney
Book, the best of the American Tourney publi-
cations, both in point of games and annotations:

Black—2, 3, 5, 6, 7, 8, 10, 25

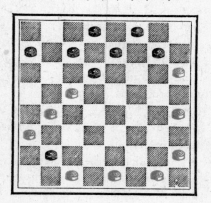

White—12, 14, 17, 20, 21, 28, 30, 31, 32

White to play and draw

17 13	25 29	31 26	2 18	23 19
10 17	32 27	6 9	26 23	DRAWN
21 14	8 11	13 6	18 22	Jordan v.
				Ginsberg

Second Position

By Andrew Anderson

Another end-game position often met with and one which may be frequently obtained by judicious exchanges toward the close of a game. The position forms an essential part of a student's cross-board education, and should be thoroughly mastered.

Black 20, 21, King 25

White 27, 30, King 32

White to play and win

32 28	24 19	15 18	30 26	23 18
25 22	18 22	17 13	9 14	10 6
28 24	19 15	18 22	26 23	18 14
22 18	22 17	13 9	14 10	6 1

14	9	9	14	1	6	14	9	15	19
1	5	27	23	5	1	23	18	29	25
9	6	14	10	6	9	9	5	27	32
5	1	23	18	1	5	18	14	25	22
6	2	10	6	9	14	5	1	19	24
1	5	18	14	5	1	14	9	20	27
2	6	6	1	14	18	1	5	32	23
5	1	14	9	1	5	22	17	22	17
6	10	1	5	18	23	5	14	23	18
1	5	9	6	5	9	17	10	17	13
10	15	5	9	23	27	21	25	18	14
5	9	6	1	9	14	10	15	WHITE	
15	19	9	5	19	23	25	29	WINS	

MASTER OPENING 3 — 11 15, 23 19

11 15	5 14	5 14	13 22	3 12
23 19	27 23	29 25	26 17	24 20
9 13A|	8 11	11 15	15 18	16 19
22 18	26 22	30 26	19 15	23 16
15 22	6 10	4 8	18 27	12 19
25 18	22 18c	25 22	15 8	DRAWN
10 14B	1 5D	8 11	12 16	Howe *v.*
18 9	18 9	22 17E	32 23	J. F. Horr

A. The Will o' the Wisp, one of the old stand-ard openings well known to all book-players. As it restricts the White game and eliminates all other openings arising from the 11 15, 23 19 opening, we consider it ideal for adoption by the student playing the Black pieces.

B. Very restricting, sound, draw-play, which dispenses with many complications, and though old is the favorite of a majority of the present day experts.

C. White cannot do better than run off the piece, and thus weaken the Black double corner as much as possible.

D. 14 17 would be premature, and allow White the advantage of the position.

E.   Very old sound play here is: 32 27, 3 8, 22 17, 13 22, 26 17, 2 6, 17 13, 15 18, 31 26, 18 22F, 26 17, 11 15, 23 18, 14 32, DRAWN.— Wyllie *v.* Martins.

F.   The effect of this sacrifice is startling for the moment, and at first glance it appears that Black has obtained one of those brilliant wins which make the study of the game so fascinating. White's method of escaping from the difficulty will prove instructive to the tyro.

Note

As all the ordinary Checker books contain numerous annotations on the following well-known games, which are minor variations of the above opening, we are presenting them, under their individual names, without notes, that the beginner may familiarize himself with a model line of play on each of them, while keeping firmly in mind that Master Opening 3 eliminates them all.

Minor Variation 1 — Defiance

9 142	11 15	15 24	11 18	6 15
27 233	25 22	28 19	21 17	27 23
8 11	7 11	6 9	14 21	12 19
22 18	24 20	22 18	23 5	23 16
15 22	15 24	4 8	2 6	15 19
25 9	28 19	31 27	20 16	DRAWN
5 14	11 15	8 11	10 15	Long *v.*
29 25	32 28	18 15	19 10	Duffy

Minor Variation 2 — Glasgow

8 11	3 7	9 14	6 10	10 17
22 174	28 24	22 18	27 18	25 21
11 165	7 16	14 23	10 17	19 23
24 20	24 20	17 14	25 21	26 19
16 23	16 19	10 17	1 6	17 22
27 11	25 22	21 14	21 14	DRAWN
7 16	4 8	2 7	6 10	Wyllie v.
20 11	29 25	31 27	30 25	Martins

Minor Variation 3 — Whilter

22 17	29 25	23 18	17 14	14 10
7 116	1 5	14 23	10 17	6 15
25 22	22 17	27 18	21 14	19 10
11 16	8 11	20 27	16 20	24 27
26 23	31 26	32 23	19 15	13 6
5 9	4 8	15 24	7 11	DRAWN
17 13	25 22	28 19	*23 19	Martins
3 7*	16 20	11 16	20 24	v. Wyllie

Minor Variation 4 — Tillicoultry

22 18	29 25	23 14	26 23	15 10
15 22	4 8	9 18	18 22	7 14
25 18	26 22	21 17	25 18	18 15
11 16	7 11	5 9	2 7	17 26
27 23	18 15	17 13	31 26	15 10
16 20	11 18	3 7	10 14	DRAWN
32 27	22 15	30 26	26 22	Drum-
10 14	14 18	7 10	14 17	mond

Minor Variation 5 — Old Fourteenth

4 87	15 18	11 15	8 11	9 14
17 13	24 20	28 24	26 23	31 26

Minor Variation 5—Old Fourteenth—*continued*

6	9	3	8	*13	17	12	19	7	10
13	6	30	26	22	13	22	8	25	21
2	9	9	13	8	12	14	17	17	22
26	22	19	16	*24	19	21	14	20	16
1	6	12	19	15	31	10	17	DRAWN	
32	28	23	16	26	22	8	3	Anderson	

Minor Variation 6 — Souter

6	98	15	24	18	27	5	14	3	7
17	13	28	19	32	23	25	22	21	14
2	6	11	15	10	14	1	6	15	18
25	22	27	24	19	10	31	26	22	15
8	11	*14	17	6	15	14	17	11	27
29	25	21	14	*13	9	30	25	DRAWN	
4	8	9	18	14	17	7	11	Robt.	
24	20	26	23	22	13	25	21	Martins	

Minor Variation 7 — Laird and Lady

9	139	6	10	2	6	13	17	17	21
17	14	15	6	26	22	24	19	23	18
10	17	1	17	17	26	7	10	5	9
21	1410	25	22	31	22	14	7	3	7
15	18	18	25	6	9	11	16	21	25
24	20	30	14	22	18	20	11	DRAWN	
3	8	13	17	9	13	8	22	Reed *v.*	
19	15	28	24	27	23	7	3	Schaefer	

Minor Variation 8 — Fife

5	9	24	20	13	22	29	25	8	11
26	23	15	24	25	9	1	5	22	18
9	13	28	19	6	13	25	22	2	6

Minor Variation—8 Fife—*continued*

31 26	6 10	32 27	7 10	23 18
13 17	23 18	4 8	14 7	10 14
21 14	17 21	18 15	3 10	DRAWN
10 17	27 23	11 18	27 23	Wyllie *v.*
18 14	10 17	23 14	5 9	Yates

Minor Variation 9 — Alma

3 8	16 30	12 16	6 9	2 11
25 22	31 26	17 13	13 6	16 7
11 16	30 23	9 14	1 26	4 8
26 23	27 18	24 20	27 23	7 3
7 11	11 15	16 19	26 30	8 12
30 26	18 11	32 27	23 16	DRAWN
15 18	8 15	14 17	15 19	Banks *v.*
23 7	7 3	21 14	3 7	Jordan

Minor Variation 10 — Black Doctor

19 10	29 25	22 15	*22 15	19 1
7 14	1 6	11 27	11 18	17 22
27 23	32 27	*31 24	21 14	26 17
4 8	6 9	10 14	*13 17	13 29
25 22	27 24	25 22	20 16	DRAWN
3 7	2 6	7 11	9 13	Sturges
24 20	24 19	30 25	16 11	in An-
6 10	14 18	14 18	8 15	alysis

———————×———————

Major Variation 3-A — 11 15, 24 19

11 15	9 14B	5 14	15 24	1 5
24 19A	22 18C	25 22E	28 19	18 9
15 24	7 11D	11 15	8 11	G5 14
28 19	18 9	32 28F	22 18	29 25

Major Variation 3-A—*continued*

4 8	22 18	8 11	19 15	DRAWN
25 22	15 22	30 26	11 18	Various
11 15	26 17	6 9	17 13H	Authors

A. The Second Double Corner, a favorite of the late C. H. Freeman, a noted American expert, which forms an equal and interesting game.

B. 8 11 has been more usual in the past, and leads to well-known and sound continuations. The reader is referred to Lee's Guide and other standard works.

C. A good alternative is 22 17 at this point, for which play see Major Variation 4-B.

D. An old line, which will return to favor when the value of transpositions is more appreciated by the average player. In 4-B the position at this point is reached by playing **7 10** in place of 7 11.

E. The late Mr. Freeman, referred to in Note **A**, was particularly partial to the Second Double Corner game, and in a match with Mr. J. Wyllie, one of the fathers of the game, varied here with: 26 22, 11 15, 27 24, 8 11, 22 18, 15 22, 25 9, 6 13, 29 25, 11 15, 25 22, 1 5, 32 28, 4 8, 24 20, 15 24, 28 19, 8 11, 22 18, 3 7, 18 14, 10 17, 21 14, 13 17, 31 26, 11 16, 20 11, 7 16, DRAWN.—J. Wyllie *v.* C. H. Freeman.

F. Many years ago and continuing for quite a period of time, the Second Double Corner was considered a loss for White, and when a draw was found which was considered playable, so weak as to merit the disfavor of the players of the day. We presume this was caused by the fact that the player of the White pieces never considered breaking his bridge, which is known generally as a strong element in the game. In this particular case, it happens to be an exception to the rule, and the occupation of the key-square is superior to holding the bridge-position.

G. Black follows White's lead in occupying his key-square, and the positions are equal.

H. A sound draw throughout.

Major Variation 3-B — 11 15, 23 18

11 15	26 19	5 9	31 24	10 15
23 18A	11 16E	26 23	1 5	8 3
8 11B	19 15	3 8	24 20	15 22
27 23	9 13F, G	24 19	2 7	23 19
10 14C	32 27	8 24	22 17	14 17
23 19D	16 20	28 12	13 22	21 14
14 23	30 26	6 10H	25 18	DRAWN
19 10	12 16	27 24	7 11	Wyllie *v.*
7 14	15 11	20 27	12 8	Bryden

A. An old-line opening named the Cross, from which many beautiful games and fascinating shots arise.

B. The Transposition Tables show that if 7 11 be played here we have Master Opening 4 at third move, thus making one line of play cover two opening formations.

C. If 4 8, 23 19, 9 14, 18 9, 5 14, 22 17, 6 9, 25 22, 9 13 and we have the 25 22 line of the Old Fourteenth, and old standard opening, which, while not exhausted, is panting for breath.

D. Many experts have shown a preference for 22 17 here, the play running: 22 17, 15 22, 17 10, 6 15, 25 18, 15 22, 26 17, 11 15, 17 13, 9 14, 24 19, 15 24, 28 19, 7 10, 29 25, 4 8, 25 22, 8 11, 22 18, 3 7, 18 9, 5 14, 30 26, 2 6, 26 22, 14 17, 21 14, 10 26, 31 22, 7 10, 32 28, 11 16, 22 17, 10 14, DRAWN.—Published Play.

E. 1 6 was played to a drawn result in the Third American Tourney.

F. 3 8, 30 26, 14 18, 32 27, 16 19, 21 17, 12 16, 25 21, 18 25, 29 22, 16 20, 17 13, 8 12, 22 18, 4 8, *15 10 leading to a drawn game. This is the famous 3 8 line of the Cross, made famous by Mr. Simeon Crumb of Boston, U. S. A.

G. Another alternative here is: 4 8, 24 20, 16 19, 20 16, 2 7, 30 26, 14 18, 32 27, 9 13, 27 23, 18 27, 31 24, 5 9, 24 20, 7 11, 16 7, 3 10, 20 16, 10 14, 16 11, 14 18, 11 4, 18 23, 4 8, 23 30, 8 11, 1 5, 11 7, 30 26, 7 10, 26 17, 21 14, 9 18, 10 1, 13 17, 1 6, 17 21, 25 22, 18 25, 29 22, 21 25, DRAWN.—Published Play.

H. 2 7, 22 17, 13 22, 25 18, *6 10 also draws, but if 1 5 is played instead of 6 10, Black loses

by *18 15, 9 13, 29 25, 7 11, 15 8, 4 11, 12 8,
etc., WHITE WINS.—Gardner v. Hynd.

Major Variation 3-C — 11 15, 22 18

11 15	9 13	6 10E	3 7	14 17
22 18A	25 22	28 24	18 11	21 14
15 22	4 8	1 5F	7 23	10 26
25 18	23 18	*23 19	31 26	30 23
10 15B	8 11	11 16	9 14	
18 11	27 23	20 11	26 19	DRAWN
8 15	5 9	7 23	2 7	Published
29 25C	24 20D	26 19	24 20	Play

A. The Single Corner opening, the name being
derived from the opening moves on each side
being from each single corner, and so called in
Anderson's Second Edition on the game. The
books give more supposedly different variations
on this than on any other opening, the number
running into the thousands. It is perhaps the
most popular way to start play between inexperienced players, the reason perhaps being that an
exchange is made at the very beginning, something particularly pleasing to the tyro.

B. This makes the formation counterpart with
a 10 15, 22 18 opening formation, but 12 16 and
8 11 have both been greater favorites than our
text, which, however, attains the object of all
scientific play, a sound draw. If 12 16 White
replies with 18 14, eliminating a few thousand
variations including the Flora Temple; if 8 11,

23 19 and the position is now a Tillicoultry opening, a minor variation of Master Opening Three.

C. 21 17 has some adherents, in reply Black
plays 9 13, a strong move leading to many delicate and deceptive endings. We give a line of
the play for examination: 21 17, 9 13, 30 25,
13 22, 25 11, 7 16, 24 20, 3 8, 20 11, 8 15, 28 24,
4 8, 24 20, 8 11, 27 24, 5 9, 32 28, 9 14, *24 19,
15 24, 28 19, 14 17, 19 16, 12 19, 23 7, 2 11,
26 23, 17 22, 23 19, 11 15, 19 10, 6 15, 20 16,
15 19, 16 11, 19 23, 11 7, 23 26, 7 2, 26 30, 2 7,
30 25, 31 26, 22 31, 29 22, DRAWN.—Jordan *v.*
Cain.

D. 24 19 also leads to draw play, but is
rather hazardous for beginners.

E. Defending key-square 14 is superior to
attacking by 15 19, which allows White winning
opportunities.

F. Very old, but sound play here is: 10 14,
22 17, 13 22, 26 10, 7 14, 30 26, 15 22, 26 10,
2 7, 24 19, 7 14, 31 26, 1 5, 19 16, DRAWN.—
J. Sturges.

Major Variation 3-D — 11 15, 21 17

11 15	17 14D	13 22	25 21	11 18
21 17A	10 17	26 17E	15 19	30 25
9 13	21 14	4 8F	23 16	8 11
25 21B	6 10	29 25	12 19	31 26
8 11C	22 17	1 6	24 15	11 15

Major Variation 3-D—*continued*

28 24	10 19	21 17	6 10	DRAWN
15 19	17 13	8 12	27 23	Jordan
24 15	3 8	25 21	18 27	*v.* Banks

A. The Switcher, a standard opening in which White has all the work to do. It was originally introduced by the great James Wyllie in one of his numerous matches, was named by him, and as he put it, he subsequently "switched many an opponent with it."

B. 22 18 is not recommended, as it results in a feeble game for White. The text is best and prepares for the exchange two moves later.

C. There is also published play on 5 9 and 6 9 here, which delay the exchange, but are not considered as strong as the text.

D. This is unquestionably White's strongest move. 30 25, an old line conceded to be weak for the second player, has been sweeping the country, but does not compare favorably for strength with our text. An example of the 30 25 line: 30 25, 4 8, *24 19, 15 24, 28 19, 11 15, 17 14, 15 24, 27 20, 10 17, 21 14, 8 11, 32 28, 6 10, 25 21, 10 17, 21 14, 1 6, 29 25, 6 10, 25 21, 10 17, 21 14, 2 6, 22 18, etc., DRAWN.—Lieber *v.* Cameron, 1923 Cedar Point Tourney. If 11 16 is played at sixth move of this note the play runs into a line of 3-A.

E. The ability to obtain this strong hold on White is what makes the opening so strong for Black.

F. 15 18 is old but good here: 15 18, *24 20**G**, 3 8, 29 25, 1 6, 28 24, 18 22, 25 18, 11 16, 20 11, 8 22, 32 28, 4 8, 24 20, 6 9, 28 24, 9 18, 23 14, 10 15, 17 13, 8 11, 27 23, 12 16, 13 9, 15 18, 9 6**H**, 2 9 or 18 27, DRAWN.—Published Play.

G. The student should memorize the following: After 26 17 is played if Black plays 3 8, 4 8, 2 6, or 1 6, the correct White reply is 29 25, but against 15 18, *24 20 is a star move. The 3 8 line given in Note F is very strong for Black.

H. 24 19 is a loss, according to the old books, but as it seems natural to walk into it, we diagram the position.

We take the opportunity at this point to draw the student's attention to the fact that there are special treatises on the Switcher Opening which present exhaustive analyses on the various formations encountered, with the numerous wins and drawing possibilities. These may be most readily obtained of the recognized dealers in checker literature, and to the player who finds himself fascinated with the truly remarkable upsets experienced in conducting a side of this inexhaustible opening they will prove a never ending source of knowledge and enjoyment.

White—9, 14, 20, 23, 24, 30, 31

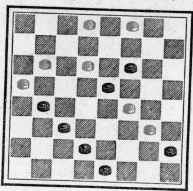

Black—2, 5, 7, 11, 16, 18, 22

White to play, and Black to win

24 19, 18 27, 19 12, 27 32, 12 8, 11 16, 20 11,
7 16, 8 3, 16 19, 3 8, 32 28, then 31 27, or 8 11,
and BLACK WINS.—Roger.

Third Position
By W. W. AVERY

In comparison with the two foregoing positions, our present study is a modern discovery, dating from a year or so previous to 1876.

The winning play is very critical and a single useless move on White's part allows the draw. The student hoping for higher honors should be well schooled in the intricacies of this fine study.

Black Kings 11, 19

White 28, Kings 12, 20

White to play and win

20 24	27 31	7 2	22 18	17 21
11 15	16 19	23 19	8 11	11 7
24 27	8 11	2 6	10 6	21 25
15 11	18 23	15 11	11 7	7 11
27 32	11 7	6 10	6 9	25 30
11 15A	19 15	11 8C	7 11	19 24
12 8	28 24	31 26	9 13	18 23
15 18B	23 27	8 11	11 7	
32 27	24 20	26 22	13 17	WHITE
19 16	27 23	11 8D	7 11	WINS

A. 19 15, 28 24, 15 10, 32 27, 10 7, 27 23, 7 3, 23 18, 3 7, 18 14, 7 3, 14 10, 11 7, 10 15, 7 2, 15 11, 2 6, 12 16, 6 2, 24 19, WHITE WINS.

B. 19 16, 28 24, 16 12E, 24 19, 15 24, 32 28, 12 3, 28 19, 3 7, 19 15, WHITE WINS.

C. 19 23, 10 14, 23 19, 14 18, 19 24, 18 23, WHITE WINS.

D. 11 15, 10 6, 15 11, 22 18, 11 7, 6 9, 7 11, 9 13, 11 7, 13 17, 7 11, 17 21, WHITE WINS.

E. 15 18, 8 12, 16 11, 12 16, 11 27, 32 14, WHITE WINS.

MASTER OPENING 4 — 10 15, 23 18

10 15	12 19	7 16	5 9E	18 22
23 18A	22 17	27 24	26 23	27 24
7 10B	9 13	6 9	*9 14F	22 26
27 23C	17 14	24 15	28 24G	24 19
3 7	11 15	9 18	10 15	14 18
32 27D	18 11	15 11	24 20	23 14
15 19	8 15	1 6	15 19	16 23
24 15	21 17	29 25	25 21	14 10
10 19	13 22	6 10	19 26	DRAWN
23 16	25 11	31 27	30 23	Tonar

A. The Kelso-Cross, a blend of two old openings.

B. 12 16 at this point is dealt with in Part Two, and, as the Transposition Tables show, may be arrived at by 12 16, 23 18, 10 15, making counterpart positions. The Tables also show that the present position in our text may be arrived at by 11 15, 23 18, 7 11, making counterpart positions, thus enabling the student to make one line of play cover two opening formations if it is desired, when handling the Black pieces, in each case.

C. We consider this best, but 26 23 also gives a sound draw and is often taken.

D. Old, but sound, and probably best. The following deviation affords a new field for the analyst:

24 20	18 15	20 11	24 15	15 10
9 13	11 18	6 10	2 6	23 19
28 24	22 15	15 6	1 10	10 7
15 19	13 22	8 29	9 14	8 11
24 15	25 18	6 1	10 17	7 3
10 19	7 11	9 13	13 31	11 15
23 16	32 28	31 27	28 24	3 8
12 19	1 5	4 8	31 27	DRAWN
21 17	29 25	27 24	24 20	Stewart
5 9	11 16	5 9	27 23	v. Banks

E. The position is highly instructive at this point and worthy of a little study. 10 15 also draws here.

F. 10 14 loses by 30 26, 9 13, 26 22, 14 17, 22 15, 17 21, 25 22, 21 25, 22 18, 25 30, 11 8, and WHITE WINS.—J. Tonar.

G. If 30 26 Black replies with 10 15, then 25 21 or 28 24, and the game may be abandoned as drawn.

Part Two, Master Opening 4 — 10 15, 23 18

10 15	21 17	11 16	32 28F	19 26
23 18	9 13	25 21	*9 14G	31 22
12 16A	17 14	1 6	18 9	16 19
26 23B	6 9	19 15	5 14	#21 17
8 12C	24 19E	7 10	22 17	DRAWN
30 26D	15 24	14 7	13 22	Published
16 20	28 19	3 19	26 1	Play

A. This is perhaps the oldest known continuation in the Kelso-Cross Opening.

B. The modern reply, original we believe with Mr. N. W. Banks, American Match Champion. 21 17 has held the limelight for many years, and although it has been subjected to intense analysis, it still is the favorite with many players.

C. In our opinion this is best, although 16 20 is playable and 16 19 has become almost the accepted reply to 26 23, somewhat as follows:

16 19	*22 18	6 10	25 22	15 24
23 16	15 22	24 19	8 11	28 19
11 20	25 18	9 14	30 26	1 6
18 11	4 8	18 9	11 15	
8 15	29 25	5 14	26 23	etc.,

leading to a good game for Black.

D. This move was introduced against Mr. Alfred Jordan, former English Draughts Champion, by Mr. N. McVean, and is considered superior to 24 19, which further weakens White's double corner, and allows Black a choice of 16 20, 7 10, or 9 13.

E. Mr. McVean, the Australian expert, varied here with 25 21; Mr. Jordan responded with 4 8, then 23 19, 7 10, 19 16, etc., to a drawn result.

F. Usual and best. Mr. Waterhouse employed 29 25 against Mr. Jordan in the Sixth American Tourney, but we doubt if the Boston

Cook will hold water, and would hardly advise anyone to try 29 25 on Mr. Jordan again.

G. We consider this the soundest continuation for the student. 2 7 draws, but if played may lead one into the error made by Mr. Lieberman when playing Mr. Ginsberg some years ago, as follows: 2 7, 21 17, 4 8 (7 10 instead of 4 8 loses). And the position is as follows:

Black—5, 6, 7, 8, 9, 12, 13, 16, 19, 20

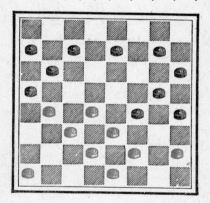

White—17, 18, 22, 23, 26, 27, 28, 29, 31

White to play and win

29 25, 19 24, 28 19, 6 10, 25 21, 7 11, 17 14, 10 17, 21 14, 11 15, 19 10, 8 11, 22 17, 13 22, 26 17, 9 13, 10 7, 13 22, 7 3, WHITE WINS.—L. C. Ginsberg.

H. The foregoing fine play is the composite product of several first-class players, and we strongly recommend its adoption by the student.

Major Variation 4-A — 10 15, 24 20

10 15	24 15	9 18	27 24	10 14
24 20A	10 19	26 23	12 19	18 9
15 19B	21 17D	19 26	22 18	15 14
23 16	11 15E	30 7	15 22	28 24
12 19	32 27	3 10	24 6	4 8
27 24c	6 10F	20 16	1 10	DRAWN
7 10	17 14G	8 12H	25 18	Various

A. A formation seldom met with under the unrestricted style of play, affording an even game for both sides.

B. Other moves are playable here, but our text is considered strongest for Black, controlling key-square 19.

C. This apparently works directly opposite to our theory of preserving the double corner, but can be classed as an exception to prove the rule, and is necessary, and White's strongest continuation from this formation. If 22 18, *6 10, *25 22, 10 14 and Black secures a powerful game. If instead of taking advantage of the situation by 6 10, Black should play 9 14, 18 9, 5 14, 25 22, then 11 15 and we have a well-known position in the 11 16, 24 20 Opening. The student will notice we star 25 22 in this note as being best for White. This is because taking the shot offered gives White a weak, if not a lost game.

D. The correct defense. 32 27, and in turn 27 24 or 27 23 lead to a very weak game for White. See Fourth American Tourney Book.

E. Nothing else seems quite so satisfactory, though there are probably other drawable moves.

F. Best, supporting the control of key-square 19. Throwing the piece by 9 14, and exchanging 19 24 with a view to capturing an extra piece and obtaining a quick king is only a mirage often seen by the beginner, as White plays 21 17, and Black is a piece short, with little possibility of drawing.

G. This shot is practically forced on White to maintain an even game. It is nevertheless sound, and hastens the game to a sound ending. It is an accepted part of the run-up.

H. Usual, but appears to hand White a quick sound draw. 10 14 seems to be a little better, while 8 11 and 5 9 are probably also playable. At previous move White may go 22 18 as played between Schaefer and Searight in the International.

I. The regulation wind-up to a satisfactory draw for both players.

Major Variation 4-B — 10 15, 24 19

10 15	15 24	6 10A	9 14	11 15
24 19	28 19	22 17	25 22	27 24

Major Variation 4-B—*continued*

8	11	14	7	9	14	24	20	9	13
23	18B	3	10	18	9	15	24	*16	11
14	23	31	27	5	14	28	19	14	17
17	14B	2	6	26	23	11	15	11	7
10	17	27	18	1	5	19	16	10	14
21	14	6	9	30	26	12	19	DRAWN	
7	10C	32	28	5	9	23	16	3d A. T.	

A. If 9 14, 22 18, then 7 10, and the position is identical with Major Variation 3-A, at Note **D.** Instead of 7 10, forming the counterpart position, Black may vary with 5 9, a line which is receiving quite a little attention since Banks lost it to Stewart in their tilt for the title. A good line of play on it runs:

5	9	1	5	5	9	13	17	17	21
25	22	31	27	25	22	25	21	26	22
7	10D	12	16	9	13	8	12	21	25
19	15	27	24	22	18	14	9	19	15
10	19	16	20	24	28	6	13	11	18
23	7	24	19	30	25	21	14	22	15
14	23E	20	24	2	7	13	17		
27	18*F	18	14	18	14	15	10	DRAWN	
3	10	9	18	10	17	7	11	Ginsberg *v.*	
29	25	22	15	21	14	10	7	Henderson	

B. This odd idea has proven sound. It is credited to Mr. G. Crookston, and was introduced by Ferrie against Wyllie, and has been the accepted play since.

C. This is best. Anything else leads to questionable draws and sure losses.

D. Banks adopted 11 16 against Stewart and eventually lost the game.

E. Scientific Checkers states this take is very essential and that Henderson failed to take advantage of the fact against Ginsberg in the Third American Tourney. If our copy of the Third American Tourney is correct Mr. Henderson adopted quite a different line of play with the Blacks in the game with Ginsberg in the Third American Tourney.

F. One of Mr. Banks' rare losses in match play was chalked down in the Big Book when he captured the piece by 26 19 in his 1914 match with Mr. Jordan.

Major Variation 4-C — 10 15, 23 19

10 15	29 25	16 23	25 22G	11 16
23 19	16 23	27 11	8 11	J19 15
6 10A	26 19E	8 15	31 26H	10 26
22 17B	7 11	24 19	3 8	17 1
1 6C	17 13	15 24	32 28	26 31
25 22	11 16	28 19F	9 14	DRAWN
11 16D	22 17	4 8	26 23	J. Lees

A. Introduced by Mr. J. Wyllie playing the Black pieces against R. D. Yates in their 1876 match, and also played by Jordan against Ferrie in their match. The main body of our game is between these latter gentlemen, the last ten moves only being credited to J. Lees, who is said at the time of the Wyllie-Yates match to have derided this move. 7 10 forms the Whilter, Opening 3, Minor Variation 3.

B. Generally considered best, though 22 18 and 27 23 are also playable.

C. Maintaining the important bridge on squares 2 and 4. The text leads to a sound development. Beginners are frequently caught by the old trap: 11 16, 17 13, 16 23, 13 6, 16 23, 13 6, 2 9, 27 2, WHITE WINS. See Hill's Manual.

D. Relieving the cramp on the single corner and better than the break by 15 18.

E. Holding back the double capture and continuing the occupation of key-square 19, which is very strong.

F. The positions are now equal, though it will be seen that key-square 19 has been the cornerstone of White's defense, and while very strong is not enough to win.

G. 30 26, 8 11, 26 23, 3 7, 31 26, 11 15, 19 16, 12 19, 23 16, 7 11, 16 7, 2 11, 26 23, 11 16, 32 28, 15 19, 23 18, 16 20, 17 14, 10 17, 21 14, 19 23, 25 22, 23 26, 14 10, 6 15, 13 6, 15 19, DRAWN.— H. Freedman *v*. R. Stewart.

H. 22 18, 12 16, 19 12, 10 15, 18 14, 9 18. And we have the following beautiful problem:

Black—2, 3, 5, 6, 11, 15, 18

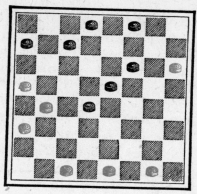

White—12, 13, 17, 21, 30, 31, 32

White to play and draw

*30 26I, *11 16, 17 14, then 18 22, DRAWN.—
H. McKean; or 2 7, DRAWN.—H. F. Shearer. At
first move of this note J. Ferrie lost to R. Jordan
as follows: 17 14, 15 19, 21 17, 11 16, 14 10, 6 15,
17 14, 18 23, 14 10, 19 24, 10 6, 2 9, 13 6, 24 27,
31 24, 16 20, BLACK WINS.—R. Jordan.

I. The position is very delicate and will repay
a little study.

J. 22 18 loses by 8 11.—J. Lees.

The continuing play for the win will be found
complete in Lees' Guide to the Game of Draughts.

Fourth Position

BY WILLIAM PAYNE

It would be difficult to calculate how many thousands of times this excellent ending has been relinquished as a draw by inexperienced players, when with proper play White could have won. Full knowledge of how to win this position is one of the milestones on the road to good playing.

Black 3, Kings 1, 2

White 12, Kings 5, 10, 11

White to play and win

or

Black to play and draw

White to play:

5	9	11	15	14	9	15	10	5	9
1	5	2	6	1	6	2	6		and
9	13	10	14	9	5	10	7		WHITE
5	1	6	2	6	1	3	10		WINS

Black to play:

2	6	14	9	6	1	5	9	A2	7
10	14	1	6	11	15	6	2		
6	2	9	13	2	6	15	10		DRAWN

A. The move is the deciding factor in this position. If White plays first he has the move, and if Black plays first *he* has it, and obtains the draw by a continuous blocking of White's attack.

10 14	23 14	7 11	26 23	22 26
22 17A	9 18	23 19	18 22	30 23
7 10B	26 23F	5 9	25 18	6 10
17 13C	10 14	19 10	15 22	29 25
3 7D	28 24	6 15	23 19	I11 16
24 20E	11 15G	13 6	1 6	Published
14 18	31 26H	2 9	32 28	Play

A. The Denny, named by Mr. Strickland. An old-line opening slightly in favor of White.

B. Supporting key-square 14. 14 18 will probably draw, but is considered weak at this point. A few of the old masters showed a preference here for 6 10, now seldom played.

C. 24 19 leads to an even game, as played by J. Ferrie in the 1912 Scottish Championship games. Reynolds tried it on Jordan in the Fifth American Tourney with a drawn result.

D. It will be noted Black has two triangle formations, one supporting an attack to be launched from key-square 14, the other acting as a defense measure. 11 15 is weak.

E. 25 22 is also favored by modern experts, notably N. W. Banks, with whom it is a favorite.

24 19 is also playable, but not recommended. The 25 22 line: 25 22, 14 17, 21 14, 9 25, 29 22, 11 15, 24 20, 7 11, 23 18, 12 16, 27 23, 15 19, 30 25, 10 15, 25 21, 5 9, 32 27, 6 10, 13 6, 2 9, 21 17, 8 12, 27 24, *4 8, 17 14, 10 17, 22 6, 15 22, 26 17, 19 26, 31 22, 1 10, 22 18, 10 15, 18 14, 15 18, DRAWN.—Schmutz's Manuscript (from Published Play).

F. The usual defense in the past, cramping Black's double corner and key-square 14. 21 17 is fast growing in popularity, practically forcing 10 15. The play: 21 17, *10 15, 26 23, 18 22, 25 18, 15 22, 23 18, 6 10, 30 25, 1 6, 27 23, 10 15, 28 24, 12 16, 17 14, etc., and the draw is practically assured. The last seven moves of this note are an innovation of W. E. Davis of the Wells Memorial Club in Boston, Mass.

G. 6 10, *31 26, 1 6, 25 22, 18 25, 29 22, 14 17, 21 14, 10 17, 23 19, *6 10, 27 23, 11 16, 20 11, 7 16, 23 18, 16 23, 26 19, 17 26, 30 21, 8 11, etc., DRAWN.—Reynolds *v.* A. Jordan. The starred move, *31 26, was introduced by C. F. Barker against R. Jordan.

H. 30 26, 8 11, 23 19, 6 10, 26 23, 1 6, 21 17, 14 30, 23 14, 10 17, 19 1, or 19 3, DRAWN.—Published Play. A good line.

I. The ending is worthy of study:

Black—4, 8, 9, 10, 12, 14, 16

White—19, 20, 21, 23, 24, 25, 27, 28

White to jump and draw

Continue: 20 11, 8 15, 25 22, 4 8, 21 17, 14 21, 22 17, 9 13, DRAWN.—Third American Tourney (Annotations).

Major Variation 5-A — 10 14, 24 20

10	14	23	18 F	4	8	31	27	7	14
24	20 A	14	23	29	25	6	9	27	24
11	15 B	27	11	15	19	27	23	*3	7
22	17 C	8	15	25	21	12	16 G	24	8
6	10	17	14	8	11	*32	27 H	7	10
25	22 D	10	17	22	18	13	17	DRAWN	
9	13 E	21	14	1	6	14	10 I	F. Dunne	

A. The Denny-Lassie, a restricted opening formation which, like some others, may be run into old-time play when you have a fair knowledge of transpositions. The opening moves are productive of many interesting formations and positions.

B. An effort to secure the center. If 6 10, 22 18, 10 15, 28 24, 15 22, 26 10, 7 14, 25 22, 1 6, and we arrive at a position which can also be obtained from Master Opening 6, as follows: 9 14, 22 18, 5 9, 24 20, 10 15, 28 24, 15 22, 26 10, 7 14, 25 22, 1 5, and the positions are now counterpart.

C. 22 18 enjoys equal favor here, for play, on which see Part Two, immediately following. 28 24 also has some advocates, but we recommend our text as best.

D. 17 13, 1 6, 28 24, 8 11, 23 19, 15 18, 26 23, 4 8, and the position is now a well-known variation of the regular Lassie.

E. Though not as strong as our text, the 14 18 cut is a natural reply here, and is drawable.

F. This is necessary to maintain equality of position.

G. We especially favor this as making a beautiful and tricky ending; although 11 15 also draws:

8

Black—2, 3, 5, 7, 9, 11, 12, 13, 19

White—14, 18, 20, 21, 23, 26, 28, 30, 32

Black to play and White to draw

11 15, 18 11, 9 27, 32 16, 12 19, 26 23, 19 26, 30 23, 7 16, 20 11, 2 6, 28 24, 5 9, etc., DRAWN.— Parry *v.* Goldsboro.

H. Highly important. If 30 25, 13 17, 25 22, 11 15, 22 6, 15 31, 20 11, 19 26, 6 1, 7 16, 32 27, 31 24, 28 12, 26 30, 21 17, 30 25, BLACK WINS.— Frank Dunne.

I. 27 24 loses by 11 15, 18 11, 9 27, 21 14, 27 31, 24 15, 31 22, BLACK WINS.

Many games are lost by players with a fair knowledge of the openings through inattention to the endings.

10 14	10 15	8 24	2 7	10 17
24 20	24 19	28 19	18 9	26 23
11 15	15 24	4 8	5 14	17 26
22 18**J**	28 19	18 15	25 22	31 22
15 22	7 10	9 13	11 15	7 10
25 18**K**	32 28	15 6	19 16	16 12
6 10**L**	3 8	1 10	12 19	10 14
26 22	30 26	29 25	23 16	DRAWN
8 11	11 16**M**	8 11	14 17	A. Jordan
27 24	20 11	22 18	21 14	*v.* Banks

J. Equal in strength and popularity with the
22 17 reply. It is also a very natural move,
obtaining command of the center.

K. The double take by 26 10 was once very
fashionable, and is still played occasionally for
the sake of a little variety, although it allows
Black great restrictive opportunities if taken:

26 10	11 15	18 9	5 14	31 22
7 14*	29 25	5 14	30 26	11 16
25 22	15 24	25 22	3 7	20 11
6 10	28 19	8 11	26 22	7 16
23 19	4 8	22 18	14 17	19 15
8 11	22 18	1 5	21 14	DRAWN
27 23	9 13	18 9	10 26	Pub. Play

L. Conservative, and holds White in strong
check. 12 16 was in style for some years, but
our text is now considered best. 7 10, however,
affords ample field for analysis as played by Banks
v. Jordan in their 1917 match. We give the play
that the lines may be compared by the student:

7 10	27 24	15 24	32 28	8 24
26 22	10 15	28 19	11 16	28 19
8 11	24 19	3 8	20 11	4 8

and here Jordan ventured 31 27 with fatal results, but a little examination seems to show 19 15 as the move to equalize the game.

M. 11 15 or 11 16 is optional, as both lead to a drawn game.

Major Variation 5-B — 10 14, 24 19

10 14	5 14	2 6H	8 15	6 10
24 19A	*26 22D	25 22I	22 17	9 6
6 10	11 15	16 20J	15 18	10 14
22 17B	*22 17E	23 18K	17 14	32 28
9 13C	*7 11F	14 23	10 17	1 10
28 24	*29 25G	27 11	21 14	19 16
13 22	11 16	20 27	18 23	DRAWN
25 9C	17 13G	31 24	14 9	Dunne

A. One of the modern Two-Move-Restriction opening formations, slightly favoring White.

B. Attacking Black's double corner, and is strongest. 22 18 has received some attention from the experts and leads to a drawable game.

C. The accepted continuation, and proven best.

D. Strongest, 29 25 also draws, but is not as forceful.

E. If 29 25 now and Black would probably take the two for two cut, which White should not allow.

F. 8 11 is an old continuation, now practically discarded.

G. We recommend this as best, although 17 13, 2 6, 30 25, also leads to a good game for White.

H. The preferred move, but 1 6 also draws.

I. 30 26 is a new departure here, which has much to commend it, although it breaks White's bridge, which seems permissible due to the formation at this point:

Black—1, 3, 4, 6, 8, 10, 12, 14, 15, 16

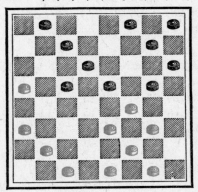

White—13, 19, 21, 23, 24, 25, 27, 30, 31, 32

White to play and win

30 26	3 8	22 18	11 15	24 20
8 11L	28 19	15 22	23 19	14 18
24 20	11 15	26 17	15 18	11 7
15 24	20 11	4 8	20 16	WHITE
25 22	15 24	31 27	18 23	WINS
1 5	27 20	8 11	16 11	Banks *v.*
32 28	8 15	27 24	23 27	Stewart

J. 8 11 is an old "snap" which has been the downfall of many a novice: 8 11, 24 20, 15 24, 23 19, 16 23, 27 2, WHITE WINS.—Published Play.

K. Necessary to break up the cramped position. If 32 28 or 30 or 31 26, Black gets in 8 11 and 11 16 with winning possibilities.

L. Looks like the loser. 16 20, 32 28, 3 7, 25 22, 8 11, 19 16, 12 19, 23 16, 14 17, 21 14, 10 17, 26 23, 17 26, 31 22, 7 10 probably draws. —R. Stewart.

Major Variation 5-C — 10 14, 23 19

10 14	5 14	5 14	2 6	16 23
23 19A	29 25	30 25	31 26	27 18
11 16	7 11	11 15	11 16F	20 27
26 23B	25 22E	25 22	26 22G	32 23
9 13C	6 10	16 20	15 18	3 26
22 17D	22 18	22 17	22 15	DRAWN
13 22	1 5	8 11	14 18	Wende-
25 9	18 9	17 13	23 7	muth

A. An opening formation leading to many beautiful combinations.

B. Supporting key-square 19 and strongest. 22 17 has been played many times. It allows Black a very easy game. 27 23 is sound and 19 15 makes a good game. We present play on it:

19 15	18 25	15 10	5 14	7 11
7 11H, I	29 22	6 15	22 18	15 19
24 20	9 13	17 14	14 23	11 16
11 18	27 23	8 12	28 24	19 24
22 15	3 7	*27 23J	19 28	16 19
16 19	23 16	2 7	26 3	32 28
25 22	12 19	23 16	28 32	20 16
14 18	32 27	12 19	3 7	DRAWN
21 17	7 11	14 9	11 15	Dunne

C. 6 10 here is equally strong, and is favored by many players. The student will note that the position at this point, as the Transposition Tables show, may also be arrived at from 9 13, 23 19, 11 16, 26 23, and then 10 14, making counterpart positions.

D. 24 20 allows the old "snuffer" that has caused many a beginner to sneeze: 24 20, 14 17, 21 14, 6 10, 20 11, 10 26, 31 22, 8 31, and BLACK WINS.

E. Beware of 24 20 here also. Black plays 14 18 and wins.—F. R. Wendemuth.

F. The following correction of recent analysis of old play is here noted:

12 16	16 19	7 16	22 26	26 31
19 12	23 16	24 19	6 2	DRAWN
11 16	3 7	16 23	15 19	Smith
13 9K	22 18	27 9	31 27	Hart
6 13	15 22	10 15	4 8L	Lawrence
26 22	16 11	9 6	12 3	et. al.

G. Banks and Jordan played 21 17, 14 21, 26 22, 21 25, 22 17, 25 30, 17 14, 10 17, 19 1, etc., to a drawn result.

H. Although old, the following alternative is equally good:

16 20I	22 15	11 18	31 27	1 5
22 17	3 7N	27 24	15 19	10 7
7 11M	28 19	20 27	17 14	5 9
17 10	8 11	32 7	9 18	27 23
11 18	15 8	2 11	22 15	
26 22	4 11	25 22	5 9	
6 15	21 17	11 15	15 10	DRAWN
24 19	7 10	29 25	9 14	Brown v.
15 24	19 15	12 16	25 22	Harrower

I. 14 18, 24 20, 16 19, 22 17, 9 13, 17 14, *7 11, leads to a sound draw.

J. 30 25 loses here. The position is diagrammed for the enlightenment of the student. Mr. Hugh Henderson, who evolved the winning play, was a naturalized citizen who had made America his home for a number of years prior to his death. He became fascinated with the game at an early age and developed into one of the finest players in Great Britain, obtaining many high honors before settling in Pennsylvania.

White—14, 20, 22, 25, 26, 27, 28, 31

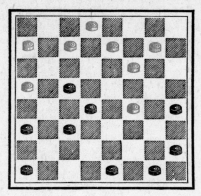

Black—1, 2, 4, 5, 11, 12, 13, 15, 19

Black to play and win

1 6, 14 10, 6 9, 10 7, 4 8, 20 16, 11 20, 27 23,
2 11, 23 7, 8 11, 28 24, 20 27, 31 24, 11 16, 24 20,
16 19, 7 3, 19 24, BLACK WINS.—Hugh Henderson.

K. 12 8 is also very good, but not of sufficient
strength to win:

12 8	26 22	22 18	6 2	28 19
3 12	16 19	15 22	26 31	DRAWN
13 9	23 16	24 6	2 7	Lieber-
6 13	12 19	22 26	31 24	man

L. If Black fails to throw the piece first, and
plays 26 31 at once, White scores by 2 7, 31 24,
12 8, and WHITE WINS.—J. E. Green.

M. We consider this strongest for Black here. The following game occurred in an English Correspondence Tourney:

14	18	8	11	3	8	20	27	17	22
24	19	26	22	10	7	32	23	14	10
7	11	4	8	15	18	22	26	25	30
28	24	22	15	22	15	14	9	9	6
11	16	11	18	11	18	5	14	22	26
17	14	25	22	7	3	18	9	6	2
16	23	18	25	8	11	*12	16	26	31
26	19	29	22	3	7	23	18	2	7
2	7	8	11	11	16	*26	30	31	26
30	26	31	26	7	10	18	14	23	27
9	13	11	15	16	23	13	17		
15	10	26	23	10	15	15	18		
6	15	7	11	18	22	30	25	DRAWN
19	10	23	19	27	18	18	23	Buchanan

N. 1 6 also draws as played by Banks against various players.

Major Variation 5-D — 10 14, 23 18

10	14	*6	10c, D	15	22	15	24	8	11
23	18A	30	26	25	18	28	19	19	16
14	23	11	15	9	14	4	8	12	19
27	18	18	11	18	9	29	25	23	7
12	16B	8	15	5	14	8	12	2	11
32	27	23	18E	24	19	25	22	*26	23
16	20B	7	11	11	15	3	8	DRAWN
26	23	22	17F	26	23	31	26	J. F. Horr

A. The most equal of the four previously barred openings. Examination shows that while

Black has an advantage, it is so slight as to be
practically negligible. In fact, White with the
weak side in this so-called barred opening, has
far better chances of drawing than Black does
with the weak side in the Edinburgh (Master
Opening 7). Although "comparisons are odious,"
nevertheless if this opening is weak enough to be
barred, then the Edinburgh should be thrown out
entirely. In our opinion, the early masters "mis-
cued" in barring this opening formation and
allowing the Edinburgh to remain.

B. Best in three of the four barred openings,
continuing the attack on White's weakened double
corner.

C. Now considered slightly superior to the
older continuation by 11 15. In the Fourth
American Tourney the following was played:

7 10d	22 18	4 8	18 11	10 17
30 26	*15 24	22 18	7 16	21 14
9 14	18 9	3 7	22 17	1 5
18 9	6 13	29 25	13 22	19 15
5 14	28 19	8 11	26 17	DRAWN
24 19	8 12	25 22	2 6	Hanson v.
11 15	25 22	11 15	17 14	Bradford

D. The following is taken from Checker
Classics:

11 16	6 9	7 11	3 10	10 14
21 17	18 15	15 8	*25 22	24 19
8 12	9 18	4 11	*2 6	11 15
30 26	23 14	26 23	29 25	19 10
9 13	1 6	6 10	*6 9	DRAWN
17 14	22 18	14 7	25 21	E. A. Smith

E. White's strongest move at this point.—
J. F. Horr.

F. Improves published play where 18 14 is
given.—J. F. Horr.

Fifth Position

AUTHOR UNKNOWN

As it is not known to whom credit is due for
this excellent position, Mr. F. Tescheleit of London some years ago suggested the title by which
it is now known.

It once again serves to illustrate the inner
beauties of scientific Checkers, and as it may be
arrived at from various games, is exceedingly useful in escaping from an apparently lost game.
While not very difficult, the student will do well
to file it in his "mental" library.

The obvious fact that one or more pieces must
be sacrificed to continue the game plays a leading
part in encompassing the downfall of the inexperienced player. Having been shaken from a
methodical train of thought, all the player's plans
are now disturbed, with the result that an
incorrect sacrifice is most often made.

Black 10, 11, 12, 13, 14

White 19, 20, 21, 22, 27

White to play and draw.

20 16	22 18	9 6	2 6	19 15
11 20	24 27	27 31	27 18	18 11
27 23	18 9	6 2	6 9	9 18
20 24	10 14**A**	31 27	13 17	**DRAWN**

A. If Black should decide to play 27 31 at this point, then White can still draw by 23 18, 31 27, 18 14, 10 17, 21 14. DRAWN.

MASTER OPENING 6 — 9 14, 22 18

9	14A	12	16	1	5C	10	19	3	7
22	18	28	24	32	28	24	15	F22	17
5	9	16	20	7	11	16	19	7	10
24	20B	24	19	*27	24D	23	16	28	24
11	16	4	8	20	27	12	19		
20	11	29	25	31	24	*26	23	DRAWN	
8	22	8	12	11	16	19	26	Drum-	
25	18	25	22	*19	15E	30	23	mond	

A. The Double Corner game, a sound and interesting game, in which Black occupies key-square 14 from beginning to end of game.

B. 25 22 is also very strong. As the Transposition Tables show, this position may also be arrived at by 9 14, 24 20, 5 9, 22 18, making counterpart positions.

C. Breaking the bridge to support key-square 14, which makes Black's game very strong.

D. The sequel to Note **C.** This exchange is forced to maintain an equal game.

E. White must break the tension. 24 20 now loses by 3 7, and after the exchange there is nothing left.

F. Accurate timing is most essential; 28 24 here, which would be two moves ahead of time, loses by 9 13. Many players, not carrying watches, have lost this.

PART TWO

9 14	8 11	16 20	7 14	13 17
22 18	22 18H	23 19	26 23	K19 16
5 9	11 16	20 27	3 7	12 28
24 19G	29 25	19 10	24 20	23 19
11 15*	7 11	14 23	7 10	14 23
18 11	25 22I	26 19	32 27	21 7
8 24	10 15	9 13	1 5	9 13
28 19	19 10	31 24	27 24	DRAWN
4 8	6 15	2 7J	5 9	Nelson v.
25 22	27 24	*30 26	22 18	Jordan

G. An ancient line now in favor, forcing Black to exchange to maintain an equal game. 11 16 is weak.

H. White now appears best.

I. R. Jordan introduced 18 15 against J. Ferrie, with a drawn result.

J. Black regains the piece necessary to draw.

K. The famous Cowan's Coup, drawing an apparent loss, and makes a dandy problem position:

Black—9, 10, 11, 12, 14, 17

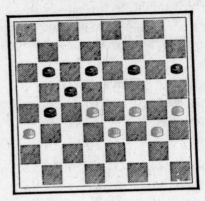

White—18, 19, 20, 21, 23, 24

White to play and draw

Major Variation 6-A — 9 14, 23 18

9 14	6 9	9 14	7 16	2 6
23 18**A**	14 10**D**	29 25	27 23	19 10
14 23	7 14	8 11	5 9	6 15
27 18**B**	22 18	32 27	28 24	30 26
12 16**C**	14 23	11 16	16 20	9 13
18 14	26 12**E**	24 20	23 19	DRAWN
10 17	11 15	3 7	20 27	Jordan
21 14	25 22	20 11	31 24	*v.* Horr

A. Another of the four heretofore Barred Openings, still under heavy fire by the experts, with the definite result, like the others in question, still in doubt, though it seems to afford a more equal game than 11 or 12 16, 23 19.

B. Little exploration has been made on the 26 19 take, but few can be discovered who recommend it.

C. Black attacks White's broken triangle and key-square 19. At this point we desire to state that the author does not stand sponsor for either the trunk game or any notes that may be given with regard to their reliability as to soundness of play, but gives play with an idea of furnishing the interested student a "target to shoot at." Instead of 12 16 here, we have two alternative lines of play; first, 5 9, 26 23, 12 16, 30 26, 16 20, 24 19, 11 15, 18 11, 8 24, 28 19, 4 8, 22 18, 8 11, 32 27, 10 14, 26 22, 7 10, 18 15, 11 18, 22 15, 2 7, 25 22, 9 13, 22 18, 14 17, 21 14, 10 17, 18 14, 7 10, 14 7, 3 10, 15 11, 17 22, 11 7, 6 9, DRAWN. —Banks *v.* Lawson, Fourth American Tourney at Cedar Point, 1920. Second: 11 15, 18 11, 8 15, 22 18, 15 22, 25 18, 5 9, 29 25, 10 14, 26 23, 4 8, 24 19, 8 11, 25 22, 11 16, 18 15, 16 20, 30 26, 1 5, 22 17, 14 18, 23 14, 9 18, 28 24, 20 27, 32 14 6 10, 15 6, 2 18, DRAWN.—Long *v.* Horr, played in their 40-game match at Detroit, Mich., in 1923

D. 32 27 is understood to have proved a loss and should be avoided:

9

White—14, 22, 24, 25, 26, 27, 28, 29, 30, 31

Black—1, 2, 3, 4, 5, 7, 8, 9, 11, 16

Black to play and win

9 18, 22 15, 11 18, 26 23, 8 11, 23 14, 11 15,
30 26, 1 6, 24 20, 16 19, 27 23, 6 9, 23 16, 9 18,
28 24, 7 10, 16 11, 3 8, 25 21, 8 11, 26 22, 18 25,
29 22, 12 16, 21 17, 5 9, 17 13, 9 14, 13 9, 16 19,
9 5, 19 28, 5 1, 28 32, 1 5, 15 19, 20 16, 10 15,
5 9, 14 18, 32 27, 31 24, 19 28, 17 14, 28 32, 14 10,
15 19, 10 6, 18 22, 9 13, BLACK WINS.—Horr *v.*
Jordan, Fourth American Tourney.

E. Although, generally speaking, square 12 is
a bad spot for White to be on, throwing the piece
and taking the two for two is the accepted way
of playing this position.

Sixth Position

By A. Mackintosh

A very delicate situation frequently encountered, and as often lost by the player unfamiliar with its fine points. It was only in recent years that is was recognized as appearing in cross-board play with sufficient regularity to merit bestowing a title upon it. This is no doubt the case with all of the "Position Problems," and has proven a good idea, as it assists the student in remembering the position and playing for it when hard pressed. It is necessary that White have the "move" to draw.

Black 3, Kings 2, 15

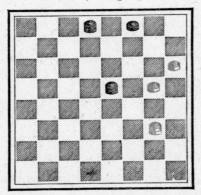

White 12, 16, King 24

White to play and draw

24 20, 2 6**A**, 20 24, 3 7, 12 8, 6 2, 8 4, **15 11**, 16 12, DRAWN.

A. 2 7, 20 24, 7 10, 24 20, 3 7**B**, 16 11, 15 8, 12 3, DRAWN.

B. 10 14, 20 24, 14 18, 24 27, 18 22, 27 31, 22 18, 31 27, 18 14, 27 24, 3 7**C**, 12 8, 15 11**D**, 8 3, DRAWN.

C. 14 10, 24 20, 10 7, 20 24, 15 11, 24 20, 11 8, 20 24, 8 4, 24 19, 7 10, 16 11, DRAWN.

D. 14 10, 8 3, 15 11, 24 20, 11 15, 16 11, 15 8, 12 3, DRAWN.

9 13	*7 10E	12 19	8 11G	10 14
22 18A	30 25F	27 24	15 8	26 22
6 9B	3 7	7 10	4 11	14 17
25 22	32 28	24 15	31 27	21 14
1 6C	15 19	10 19	6 10	H9 27
24 20D	24 15	18 15	27 23	DRAWN
10 15*	10 19	11 18	19 24	Ward v.
28 24	23 16	22 15	28 19	Coward

A. Forms the regular Edinburgh, an old-time opening, at one period styled the "New Fifteenth." It is considered very weak for Black, yet it will be found a tricky game, developing many unexpected streaks of strategy, causing both players to move with care. White's strength lies in securing control of the center with the opening move, threatening Black's key-square and double corner.

B. Strongly advocated by the author. While this move may be considered a comparatively modern continuation, there has always been much difference of opinion as to the best move for Black. 10 15 has long held the stage as the satisfactory road to a draw, with some expert losing the ending every once in a while. 11 16 is considered a

133

dead loss. 11 15 has been employed many times in important contests, with a drawn result, although well-known players do not hesitate to pronounce it a poor move, leading to a weak if not a lost game. 12 16 is the move which at present holds the fancy of the experts, many players booking up on it for no other reason than that "Bill Jones will probably play it, so I have to be familiar with it, and then besides if he plays it, and it is good enough for him, why, it is good enough for me also." To say the least, it is fortunate for the future of the game that this line of reasoning was not universal in the good old days of yore, or we would all still be playing Old Fourteenth and Single Corner. But that is by the way. This 12 16 move gives Black something like a Dundee game (Master Opening 1), and while it has its disadvantages, is workable in the majority of cases, and will no doubt be frequently encountered by the student when playing the Bill Jones type of player. A fair example of the run-up:

12 16	21 14	10 17	26 17	*5 9
24 20	16 19	21 24	6 9	20 16
8 12	24 15	18 22	29 25	*18 22
28 24	11 18	26 17	9 18	etc.
4 8	23 19	13 22	17 13	DRAWN
18 14*	6 10	30 26	2 6	Prof.
10 17	25 21	1 6	31 26	Hartshorn

C. The numerous controversies concerning the

merits and demerits of 6 9 at third move of trunk, are as nothing to the heated arguments which have arisen and continue to simmer over this move. Many players loudly proclaim it an absolute loss, and substitute 11 15 as the only hopeful continuation for a draw.

Hard work and much midnight analysis has gradually forced the fact upon us that those who frown upon 1 6, cannot get 10 15 out of their playing system and are over eager to play it as soon after the 6 9 and 1 6 moves as possible. 10 15 should only be played if White answered 1 6 with 24 20, as 10 15 is then the only correct move. See note **D**.

D. Equal in strength with 24 19, 23 19, 30 25, or 29 25. This last is perhaps the most natural continuing move for White, and we therefore offer a line of play covering it:

1 6	18 11	15 24	22 18	9 14
29 25	8 15	28 19	8 11	18 9
11 15*	24 19	4 8	27 24	5 14

and if White now follows with 24 20, we have the old and well-known Defiance game with colors reversed. The diagramed position is taken from play of a very extensive character given on this opening in F. F. Smith's 6 9 Edinburgh. This is a small pamphlet dealing exclusively with 6 9 as the second move of this opening.

Black—2, 3, 6, 7, 10, 11, 12, 13, 14

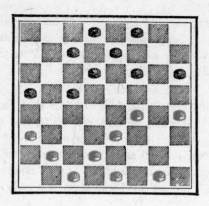

White—19, 20, 21, 23, 25, 26, 30, 31, 32

If White elects to play **25 22** instead of **24 20**, we have the following:

25 22	6 9	22 18	18 22	16 7
11 15	27 11	10 14	20 16	2 11
23 18	7 23	18 15	9 14	10 7
14 23	26 19	14 18	15 10	DRAWN
31 27	3 7	24 20	7 11	Jones

E. Best. 6 10 would permit White to develop a strong game with winning possibilities.

F. White may decide to play 23 19, whereupon Black replies with 3 7, 26 23, 9 14, etc., leading to a drawn game. **R. T. Ward. We consider the text best.**

G. A forceful move which more than assures the draw.

H. Practically all the guides and textbooks on the game, published in previous years, will give the student unlimited play on this opening, wherein Black plays 10 15 at third move of trunk. To avoid covering the same ground twice, the reader is referred to Lee's Guide, British Draughts Player, Third American Tourney Book, et al.

Major Variation 7-A — 9 13, 24 20

9 13	17 13	10 17	32 28	18 23
24 20	9 14	27 23	3 7F	26 19
11 15	29 25	7 10E	19 16	11 16
22 17A	4 8	23 19	12 19	20 11
13 22	25 22	*1 5	23 16	7 23
25 11	8 11C	31 27	17 21G	24 19
8 15	28 24	5 9	22 17	15 24
21 17B	14 18D	27 23	14 18	DRAWN
5 9	23 14	9 14	16 12	Drummond

A. The Wagram, an old line, slightly favoring White. As shown by the Transposition Tables, it is brought up from unrestricted play by the inevitable 11 15, followed by 22 17, 9 13, 24 20, 13 22 and the position is counterpart with our text at 5th move. The diagramed position is shown in order to familiarize the student with the appearance of the position brought up from either line of play.

Black—1, 2, 3, 4, 5, 6, 7, 8, 10, 12, 15, **22**

White—20, 21, 23, 25, 26, 27, 28, 29, 30, 31, 32

B. Best, attacking Black's double corner and neutralizing the effect of the previous play whereby Black gained command of the center. 29 25 is not considered so strong here, but is drawable. If 29 25, 4 8, 25 22, 5 9, 27 24, 9 14, 24 19, 15 24, 28 19, 10 15, 19 10, 6 15, the position is a regular Defiance.

C. The following deviation is both entertaining and instructive:

14 18	3 7	9 14H	11 18	18 22
23 14	23 19	25 21	19 15	27 24
10 17	1 5	7 11	10 19	
27 23	31 27	32 28	24 15	DRAWN
7 10	5 9	15 18I	2 7	Ginsberg v.
28 24	*30 25	22 15	*26 23	Henderson

D. 3 8 furnishes a restful line which assures a sound draw:

3 8ⴊ	10 14	11 25	5 14	14 23
23 18	18 9	30 21	26 23	27 18
14 23	15 19	1 5	8 11	DRAWN
27 18	24 15	31 27	23 18	Swan

E. 6 10 loses apparently, but a narrow draw is concealed in the ending:

6 10	22 17	15 18	23 18	16 23
23 18	15 18	20 16	7 11	24 19
1 5	24 19	18 27	14 7	
31 27	18 22	32 23	6 10	
2 6	26 23	3 8	7 3	WHITE
18 14	11 15	16 11	11 16	WINS
17 21	27 24	8 15ᴋ	18 11	McGill

F. The following line is given, as it is very essential that the student be familiar with the two different formations arising from 3 7 and 2 7 at this point:

2 7	15 18	11 15ᴍ	7 16	3 12
19 16	16 12	30 23	20 11	11 7
12 19	18 22	21 25	10 14	
23 16	26 23	19 16	23 19	DRAWN
17 21ʟ	22 26	14 21	15 18	Macfar-
22 17	23 19	16 11	12 8	lane

G. 14 18, 16 12, 18 25, 30 14, 10 17, 26 23, 7 10, 12 8, 10 14, 8 3, 15 18, 23 19, WHITE WINS. —Drummond.

H. The shot by 17 21, 22 17, 21 30, only draws.

I. 2 7 allows a very dramatic finish to a situation replete with thrills: 2 7, 13 9 6 13, 27 23, and WHITE WINS.—E. A. Smith.

J. 14 17 loses by 23 18, 3 8, 24 19, 15 24, 32 28, 10 14, 18 9, 7 10, 28 19, 11 15, 27 24, 1 5, 20 16, 5 14, 16 11, WHITE WINS.—W. Orrell.

K. Here is where the draw comes in: 7 16, 14 7, 16 20, etc., DRAWN.—Bjerkness.

L. Taking by 14 18 at this point has proved a very popular continuation with the experts:

14 18	26 23	21 25	2 6	19 23
16 12	17 21	9 6	26 23	9 6
18 25	23 19	25 30	19 16	DRAWN
30 14	6 10	6 2	23 19	Drum-
10 17	13 9	30 26	6 9	mond

M. If Black plays 26 31 he will find himself in a loss by a pretty little "catch" as follows.

Mr. Drummond may be classed, perhaps, as the greatest of compilers on the game. He is best known as a Single Corner analyst, having been responsible for many thousands of the variations now in use.

The collection and classification of the trunk game and variations of the Wagram, while remarkably sound and complete, was evidently merely a minor consideration in his intense study of the game, as Mr. Drummond always made the study of the Single Corner opening his specialty.

Black—3, 6, 7, 10, 11, 14, 21, 31

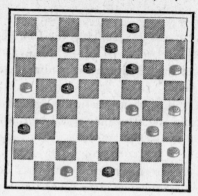

White—12, 13, 17, 19, 20, 24, 28, 30

White to play and win

12 8	24 8	28 24	20 16	24 20
3 12	31 27	23 18	14 18	18 23
19 16	8 3	3 8	8 3	17 14
12 19	27 23	18 15	15 11	

WHITE WINS.—Drummond

Major Variation 7-B — 9 13, 24 19

9 13	25 18	11 15	22 15	13 17
24 19A	9 14F	19 16	10 19	21 14
11 15B	18 9	12 19	25 22	10 17
28 24C	5 14	23 16	6 10	18 14
6 9D	24 20G	15 18H	22 18	7 11
22 18E	8 11	26 22	14 23	16 7
15 22	29 25	1 6	27 18	*3 10

Major Variation 7-B—*continued*

14 7	26 23	19 16	11 7	23 18
2 11	24 27	11 15	22 26	DRAWN
31 26	23 19	16 11	30 23	Published
19 24	27 31	17 22	31 26 ‖	Play

A. A strong White attack, almost equal in strength to 22 18.

B. 11 16 has been practically discarded, since it was found the after play could be run into the 12 16 line of Master Opening 7, and in general allows White too much scope.

C. Increases the pressure of the grip on Black. Allowing the exchange gives Black too much freedom and weakens White to some extent. If 22 18, 15 22, 25 18, we have a position which is a minor variation of Major Variation 3-C. The Transposition Tables show it may be arrived at as follows: 11 15, 22 18, 15 22, 25 18, 9 13, 24 19.

D. The recognized continuation. 8 11 appears natural but permits 23 18, after which Black is in immediate difficulty with a weak game.

E. 23 18 is also strong, and has been much favored in tourney and match play in the past. Black replies with *1 6, 18 11, 7 23, *26 19, 8 11, *24 20, leading to an even game.

F. Occupying the key-square and preventing 18 14.

G. The usual order of moves is 29 25, 8 11, and then 24 20, but 24 20 first prevents 7 11, upon which White would take two for two and give Black a bad game. 29 25 permits 7 11, and then if White plays 24 20, Black takes the two for two. If White instead plays 25 22 or 26 22, Black plays 11 15, with a comfortable game in either case.

H. The late American Champion, Mr. C. F. Barker, lost by 15 19 at this point, and it is now practically abandoned. It may draw with extremely critical play for Black, but is a hazardous line not to be recommended. 1 6 might stand some analysis, while 10 15, 27 24, 1 6, 31 26, 7 10, 16 11, 3 8, 24 19, 15 24, 22 15, 10 19, 32 28, 8 15, 26 23, and WHITE WINS.—J. G. Keenan, correcting a Gould-Ginsberg draw in the Fifth American Tourney.

I. Note carefully the method of breaking the bridge, thus assuring the draw. The knowledge will many times prove useful.

Major Variation 7-C — 9 13, 23 18

9 13	28 24G	4 8	27 24	6 9
23 18A	16 20	19 16	20 27	13 6
5 9B	18 15	12 19	31 15H	1 28
26 23C	11 18	23 16	14 18	26 22
11 16D	22 15	10 19	*29 25I	18 23
24 19E	7 10	24 15	9 14	22 18
10 14	32 28	7 11	28 24	DRAWN
30 26F	2 7	16 7	13 17	O'Grady v.
8 11	25 22	3 19	22 13	Henderson

A. An opening attack on Black's key-square and double corner, giving slightly the better of the opening, but which merges into an equal position as the game progresses.

B. Prevents 18 14, which, although strong for White, only draws.   12 16 is the move taken which allows the 18 14 cut.

C. Supporting the piece on square 18 and preparing for 30 26 five moves later.   It will be observed that White in this case is holding his bridge on squares 29 and 31.

D. The opening gun of Black's attack and development.   The exchange by 11 15, 18 11, 8 15, would permit in reply 22 18, 15 22, 15 18, giving White an almost overwhelming advantage.

E. Assures White the center and a balance in development.

F.   28 24, 16 20, 19 15, 7 11, 24 19, 3 7, 30 26, 7 10, 22 17, 13 22, 26 17, 1 5, 32 28 allows a brilliant finish.

In passing, it might be well to note that, while Mr. Priest usually plays his hardest in all games in which he participates, there are times when all players "ease up," especially when playing "amusement" games, which are comparatively unimportant and count for nothing if lost or won. Then again, Mr. Priest's age is now against him, which is admittedly a serious disadvantage.

White—15, 17, 18, 19, 21, 23, 25, 27, 28, 29, 31

Black—2, 4, 5, 6, 8, 9, 10, 11, 12, 14, 20
Black to play and win

20 24, 27 20, 9 13, 18 9, 11 27, 31 24, 13 22,
25 18, 5 23, and BLACK WINS.—E. A. Smith *v.*
M. C. Priest.

G. The accepted build-up in this formation,
although White may vary here with 22 17, 13 22,
26 10, 6 22, 25 18, 9 13, 18 14, and the position
is a straight Glasgow game with colors reversed,
brought up by the play given in Minor Variation
2 of Master Opening 3 to the Fifteenth move,
where instead of 4 8, play 9 14, and the positions
are counterpart.

H. Practically all forced play to maintain an
10

equal game, and although the play is now stereo-typed, the draw remains absolutely sound and is in favor with all the experts.

I. Only move to draw. Allowing the exchange by 18 25, 29 22, and Black plays 9 14, and White must either sacrifice the piece on 22 or allow the three for one shot.

Major Variation 7-D — 9 13, 22 17

9 13	4 8	2 6	7 10	12 16
22 17	24 19D	24 20F	18 14	11 7
13 22	15 24	10 15	9 18	16 20
25 18	28 19	19 10	22 8	7 2
6 9A	8 11	6 15	3 12	19 24
29 25B	23 18	31 26	20 16	26 23
11 15C	9 13	15 19	10 14	24 31
18 11	26 23E	23 16	16 11	DRAWN
8 15	5 9	12 19	14 18	Ginsberg v.
25 22	27 24	30 25	32 27	Henderson

A. Recommended as best for the student. 11 15 is a fairly good line, but leads to a compli-cated game. The Transposition Tables show this position may also be arrived at by 10 15, 22 18, 15 22, 25 18, 6 10 making counterpart positions.

B. This gives more possibilities for winning than the 18 14 cut, after which Black has only to continually run the piece down to obtain a draw. 26 22, though seldom played, is very good here:

26 22	8 24	29 25	11 15	18 9
10 14	28 19	4 8	32 28	5 14
24 19	9 13	25 22	15 24	31 26
7 10	30 25	3 7	28 19	11 15
22 17	13 22	27 24	7 11	DRAWN
11 15	25 9	8 11	22 18	Published
18 11	5 14	24 20	1 5	Play

C. 11 15 is now the correct continuation.

D. 21 17 and 23 18 are both playable alternatives. R. Stewart adopted the latter against Banks in their 1922 World's Championship match, with a drawn result. Our text, however, is strongest and in general favor among the experts.

E. Another sound line for White here is 27 23:

27 23	27 24	21 17	17 14	31 24
5 9	10 15	12 16	16 20	DRAWN
32 27	19 10	30 25	23 19	Published
2 6	6 15	1 5	20 27	Play

F. Try 32 28, 10 15, 19 10, 6 15, 21 17, 7 10, 23 19, and if Black fails to see the little throw by 12 16, 19 12, 1 5, and plays 1 5, immediately he casts aside the easy draw within reach and lays out some heavy labor for himself to obtain a draw.

Seventh Position

BY WILLIAM PAYNE

As the "Position Problems" appear to have received their name due to their frequent appearance in cross-board play, we propose that our present well-known study, heretofore known and referred to only as "one of Payne's draws," should be given the permanent title of Seventh Position.

It has been the means whereby thousands of apparently lost games have been drawn, and is most puzzling to the tyro and even more advanced players.

The draw for White lies in having the "move" and maintaining a king on square 22, supporting it with the second king, thus preventing the advance of the piece on square 13. Against inexperienced players White may even win the ending. The short solution given is shorn of all useless moves, but Black may try other methods of winning, which will be found unavailing against White, providing he has mastered the situation thoroughly as given here.

It might occur to the reader that a draw, such as that presented herewith, is comparatively unimportant, and it would be more to the point to so play a game that it would be unnecessary to have knowledge of such a fine draw. To such we reply that there are certain types of players who, when engaged against players of lesser ability, derive a great amount of pleasure in watching the growing mystification of the tyro. Then again, even a good player sometimes gets into unfortunate situations where this draw is needed.

Black 13, Kings 15, 17

White Kings 22, 23

White to play and draw

*23 26, 17 21, 26 23, 15 10, *23 26, 10 14, *26 30ͻ
14 17, *22 18A, *17 14B, 18 9, 13 17, DRAWN.

A. 30 26, 21 25, 22 29, 17 22, 26 17, 13 22,
BLACK WINS.

B. 17 22, 18 25, 13 17, *25 22, 17 26, 30 23,
21 17, 23 18, WHITE WINS.

PROBLEM SOLVING

The solving of problems, which incidentally familiarizes one with various positions as they arise during cross-board games, together with the correct moves necessary to complete the win or draw, as the case may be, is a highly important aid to the student's advancement as a player. It has been stated that "No one may hope to become a good player without the systematic study of problems."

Just as in games there are certain general principles to be observed, there are also certain principles involved in solving problems. The following suggestions will prove of assistance to the student taking up the serious study of problems:

1. Be sure that all pieces and kings are correctly placed, comparing the setting on your board with the figures and setting given on the diagram. Also make certain that you have towards you the side mentioned in the terms.

2. Ascertain if the forces on both sides are equal. Make certain who has the "move," as if the side named in the terms has not the move it would be policy to examine the position carefully with a view to making a judicious exchange which would change the "move."

3.   There are three main types of problems: (a) Position Problems, (b) Shot Problems, (c) Block Problems, although there are, of course, many problems which are a combination of any two or even all of the main types mentioned.

4.   The following explanation will aid in deciding to what type a problem belongs: Position problems usually have few pieces, Shot problems usually have many pieces, and Block problems, in practically every case, have one or more kings of the opposing side in the king-row of the side named in the terms.   Block problems are usually solved by shots and sacrifices.

The accompanying problems, together with the famous Position Problems appearing elsewhere in this work, have all been carefully selected for their instructive value, their usefulness, and beauty of composition.

LESSONS IN FINISHING

Selected End-Game Problems of exceptional merit, illustrating actual cross-board positions and the method of forcing a win in an apparent drawn game.

By W. Jordan

White 13, 22, 24

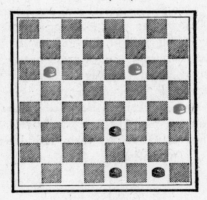

Black 1, 2, 10

Black to play and win

Solution:

1	6	19	16	6	10	11	8	26	31
24	19	14	17	16	11	22	26	3	8
10	14	22	18	17	22	8	3	31	26

B. WINS

AUTHOR UNKNOWN

White 12, 14, 26

Black 3, 5, King 6

Black to play and win

Solution:

6	9	*14	17	9	14	18	22	14	18
14	10	6	1	6	9	26	23	19	16
9	14	5	9	14	18	17	14	18	15
10	6	1	6	9	6	23	19	B. WINS

AUTHOR UNKNOWN

White 20, 21, King 27

Black Kings 14, 15, 19

Black to play and win

Solution:

19 24*	27 24	9 13	24 27	15 11
27 32	*14 9	17 14	28 24	14 10
24 28*	24 28	19 15	27 32	13 9
32 27	15 19	28 24	24 19	27 32
28 32*	21 17	32 28	32 27	19 15
				B. WINS

By George A. Rudolph
White 20, 21, 22, 32

Black 2, 5, 10, 14
Black to play and win

Solution:

5 9	2 7	18 25	25 30	23 18
32 27	16 12	8 3	10 19	16 11
9 13	*7 11c	15 18	18 23	13 17
20 16	24 20	3 7	19 26	21 14
10 15*A	*14 18D	11 15	30 23	18 9
27 24B	12 8	7 10	20 16	11 7
				B. WINS

A. 2 7, 21 17, 14 21, 22 18, 21 25, 27 23, 25 30,
23 19, 30 26, 18 15, 10 14, 15 10, DRAWN.

B. 27 23, 2 7, 16 12, 7 11, 12 8, 15 18, 22 15,
BLACK WINS.

C. 7 10, 12 8, 14 18, 22 17, 13 22, 21 17, 18 23,
8 3, 15 18, 24 19, DRAWN.

D. 15 19, 21 17, 14 21, 22 18, 21 25, 12 8,
25 30, 8 3, 30 26, 3 7, DRAWN.

GLOSSARY OF CHECKER TERMS

Alternate or **Alternative Play.** Another way to accomplish the same result; sometimes useful when it is believed an opponent is familiar with the usual line of play.

Analysis (Analyses). Trunk and branch play of a game or position. The term is not applied to compilations or annotations.

Anderson, Andrew. Accredited the "father" of modern checkers.

Annotated Game. One accompanied by notes of explanation, criticisms and suggestions.

Balloted Opening. One determined as drawn by chance from a number of agreed upon openings.

Barred Openings. Four Restricted Game Openings formerly "barred" and not played, but now generally in use by good players and dealt with exhaustively in this book.

Block. Pieces rendered unmovable by being held in solid bunch.

Book Loss. A line of play given in one or more standard works as sure to lose if properly handled by the side having the advantage.

Breeches. A king placed between two opposing pieces; either one moving, the king captures the remaining one.

Bye. A player not paired in some round of a tournament due to there being one player remaining after all others have been paired off.

Cook. Winning play previously prepared or "cooked up" for a special occasion.

Counterpart (position). A like position arrived at by a different order of moves.

Cramp or Cramped. Hard pressed for freedom of action; especially applicable to a squad of pieces on the side with no safe outlet.

Critical (position) (game). A stage of a game or solution to a problem where great nicety of play is necessary for the draw or win, usually shown on diagrams in checker books.

Cross Board Ability. What a player can see during a game.

Draw (able). A game or position admitting of a draw.

Fork. A king behind two opposing pieces, one of which cannot avoid capture, the king and pieces forming a "V."

Grip. A check on the freedom of one or more pieces.

Key Squares. See Seven Secrets of Success in Contents.

Line. All variations of a distinct branch of play regarded as a unit. A course of play producing essentially different combinations from other ways of proceeding.

Losing Move. One that starts a course of play known to end in a loss.

Man Up. One more piece in play, or ahead, than the opponent.

Manuscript. A private collection of play from all available sources.

Original Play. Not previously published.

Oversight. Failure to take advantage or opportunity to draw or win. Simple oversights are referred to as "slips."

Scientific Play. Understanding by making the correct moves in a particularly intricate situation.

Scope. Embracing more than one correct variation. A player is said to have "great scope" when there are several satisfactory ways of developing a position.

Shot (Stroke). Giving one or more pieces in order to make a long jump, usually wrecking the opponent's game.

Transposition. The same moves that produced an opening or position following one another in a different form from that given originally.

Trunk Move. A move of the trunk or main game.

Variation. Any numbered branch of play which may be traced back to the trunk, or main game. It is usual to number variations and to use letters in alphabetical sequence for notes and comments on the positions occurring in the game as played.

CHECKER HANDBOOK GAME INDEX

TWO-MOVE-RESTRICTION GAME INDEX

UNRESTRICTED GAME INDEX

NOTE.—The absence of page numbers in the Handbook Game Index indicates a transposition to some other opening previously covered. With a knowledge of the opening moves in any particular game not listed, a reference to the Transposition Tables will afford the desired information.